Sir NBBY

A Cat-ography

as told to

(and illustrated by)

LEONARD BROOKS

SIR NOBBY

A Cat-ography

as told to (and illustrated by) LEONARD BROOKS

Published in the United States by River City Publishing
1719 Mulberry Street
Montgomery, AL 36106

Designed by Lissa Monroe

First Edition—2007
Printed in
1 3 5 7 9 10 8 6 4 2

ISBN 13: 978-1-57966-079-6
ISBN 10: 1-57966-079-7

Library of Congress Cataloging-in-Publication Data:

Brooks, Leonard.
   Sir Nobby : a cat-ography / as told to Leonard Brooks. —1st ed.
     p. cm.
   ISBN 978-1-57966-079-6
   1. Cats—Poetry. I. Title. PS3602.R64445S57 2007
   811'.6—dc22
                              2007005904

Editor's Note

His name is Sir Nobby. A rather noble animal. *Hush!* I tell myself, *Don't let him hear me describe him thusly.* He is a noble Siamese. He holds his head high, his body erect, and he is very proud. Even when he sits in my lap.

Not long ago Nobby approached me about editing his memoirs, which he was constructing from his jumbled life. Having no true chronology to follow—no beginning, middle, or end as such—he had scenes of travail, remorse, triumph, and victory over some unusual circumstances. I explained that this is all you need for a well-told life. While cats have no sense of time, he does know right from wrong, good from evil, and has a trusting heart.

Nobby is a computer cat with a complicated, conceited view of his life and times that is unique. At first, I was somewhat reluctant to take on the chore and ultimate responsibility of editing his individual endeavor. But to refuse my old friend would be an affront to his haughty and high-strung personality, not to mention his high-toned sensibility. He is not accustomed to *not* having his way.

As I settled down to read his work, I became confused, then I began to fall into his unique rhythmical cadence, his ideas and words often unintelligible and catty-whompus, but still fresh and quite beautiful. As a computer cat, he is quite human, and his writing and thinking are of value. Also, they are even enlightening. With this in mind, I set about to translate my friend's life from his meowing to a more mundane form. I hope that I am successful and that you enjoy the work.

—Leonard Brooks

ACKNOWLEDGEMENTS

A grateful *meow* to all my friends who have helped me write my book. Thanks to Beverley Silverman who first suggested it to me and to the Señor for illustrating it.

A special *meow* to Wayne Greenhaw for editing and advice, and a special *purr* for making this book possible.

🐈 SIR NOBBY THE POET

I'm a new kind of a pet,
a cat for modern times.
And some of my life
I'll put on this page.
I won't have to write it,
I just jump on a mouse,
part of a computer we have in our house.

My name is Sir Nobby,
a Siamese cat
and like all my kind,
I am an aristo-cat.

I'm proud and I'm haughty
and stand out in a crowd.
I *meow* very softly,
never too loud.
I'm an artist and writer, you see.
You'll learn all about me in the story I tell.

There once was a saddened old cat
whose family was born in a hat.
And that is why,
unlike you or I,
she never can know just where she is at.

She sits on the table
or under a chair,
one time out in an ice box,
just for a careless dare.

They rescued her promptly,
then found her asleep
on the rod of an autobus,
not making a beep.

A nice comfy basket
is not what she craves,
and you'll never understand
just how she behaves.

MEOW TALK

My name is Nobby. No last name. Although I suspect it's von Hoffenbrau or something just as grand. Handsome, intelligent, spoiled as any true aristocat, I am certainly different from any thoroughbred feline you'll find in the cat population. I'm a computer-age cat, raised in a world far different from the rural atmosphere into which I was born.

This is a story of my life and times. I have known the exciting and treacherous world of Mexico, where I was born and where I have lived. Here I have managed to endure, survive, and prevail. I was born on the Gulf Coast in the rugged, industrial town of Tampico. You may remember it as the bustling roughshod frontier world in the first scenes of John Huston's classic movie, *The Treasure of the Sierra Madre*. Well, it was that kind of rambunctious world I knew as a baby kitten, and for a while it was tough going, even for one born of aristocracy. But it was not long before I found my way to a hacienda near the Gulf Coast, where I was adopted by a wonderful family who had many animals in their menagerie.

Today, I live in a world where I am revered as an individual in the beautiful Spanish colonial town of San Miguel de Allende, where many families trace their ancestry back hundreds of years to Spanish royalty. I live in a glorious garden protected by high walls. Nestled high in the mountains, we are blessed with lovely weather all year round. Here, the Señor takes care of me, loves me, and allows me to nestle in his lap in front of a roaring fire on evenings when a chilly north wind blows down upon us.

In my early life, I was not called Nobby. At first, I was simply Cat, until I escaped to the ranch. There I was called Maccabi, after the name of a chili plant that grew on the ranch belonging to the family that took me in. I thought it a rather silly name and wouldn't answer when called. With me on the coast was another cat, a nondescript animal who did not attempt to be anything but a cat. I don't even remember his name.  And there were two yapping poodle dogs who were definitely nothing but dogs. However, the dogs were obviously the favorite pets of the family.

For me, enduring such turmoil from sunup 'til nightfall was a chaotic problem that I faced daily. I found dark and dreary places to hide, curl into a ball, close my eyes, and dream of paradise. But, alas, the cat and/or the dogs would find me, create havoc, and I'd be forced to hunt for a new hiding place. Often, when I had moments to think, I plotted an escape plan that would take me to another world without plain cats and yelping poodles, where I could live peacefully among adult human beings and a few equally pleasant animals. If anything, I've always been a pleasant animal, although I do have my eccentricities. If I were a human, you might call me "a character."

Luckily, I never had to make a dangerous cross-country trek in search of paradise—although in the back of my mind such a journey was never out of the question. I was lucky because I met someone I truly liked and someone who cared for me. Into my world appeared one day a stranger who planned to stay on the ranch for a week. The guest was a very pleasant man, somewhat erudite, given to long walks alone. He was an artist who set up his easel next to the shore. Sometimes he would stand for hours, gazing at the sea and the surrounding landscape.

Watching his fluid movements, his easy gait, and the way he handled the brushes as he stroked the canvas, I knew immediately that he was someone special. When I heard his soft voice as he reached down to touch my fur, as he cooed a *meow*-voice pleasure to my ears, my back arched up to meet his fingers, and I purred a happy reply.

As he painted, I perched on a nearby stone fence that was warm to my belly. I scrunched down and eyed the man's fast-moving fingers as his brush moved across the canvas and made its empty space come alive with colorful images. What I saw in the distance, the blue-green water of the Gulf, the beige sand of the beach, and the misty breeze that fluttered through the sea oats, was reproduced quickly but accurately on the rectangle of canvas. I was amazed.

Later, after a short nap dreaming of paradise, I heard the man's *meow*-talk, saying he once had a cat like me. He said he thought my dark brown fur was a beautiful color. My eyes wide, I climbed down from the wall and made my way to the man and rubbed my side against his pants leg to show him how much I appreciated his words.

"You're a good one," the man cooed, and again I answered with a deep, throaty purr, letting him know I found him *simpatico*. "My cat was also a Siamese. He became quite famous, after I painted a portrait of him and it was reproduced in Canada and the United States, bought by thousands of people who hung him on their walls."

When the artist hiked up the beach and watched birds fluttering in the distance, I walked with him. I hid in the low-lying brush, crouching there, waiting, hoping for a bird to fly low and land nearby. If I moved quickly enough, I could grab him and hold him in my clutches and carry him to my new friend. I was sure he would like to have such a worthy gift.

In the early evening, when the artist sat on the patio and sipped his nightcap, letting his eyes feast on the sight of the setting sun reflecting off the Gulf behind us—an interesting and unusual visage of a sunset, the colors vivid but subtle in their reflection—I climbed upon his lap and lay prone. I relaxed as his gentle fingers rubbed through my hair. "You're so soft," he whispered. I purred. I closed my eyes. I did not dream of paradise. I dreamed of the man painting the sea and the shoreline and the dunes.

That night, when the man went to bed, I followed. Without asking, I lay across the bed next to him. I stretched my body as long as I could stretch it. I rolled slightly sideways, barely touching the man's backside. "You're a good boy, Nobby," the man said, and he didn't push me away.

I wondered on the name he'd called me. I'd never heard it before. *Nobby*. I had no idea what it meant. As far as I knew, it wasn't a Spanish word. But when I formed it in my cat-mind, I stood straighter, held my head higher, and stepped spryly. I liked the sound.

The next day, when the artist was preparing to leave, the owner of the ranch asked if he would like to take me with him. I would be given a veterinarian's pill and put into a basket. Then I would travel with the artist in a private plane to another part of Mexico, far away. It would be a great adventure.

I had never seen an airplane other than high in the sky over my head. At first I was afraid. I didn't

want to soar through the sky. But the Señor put my basket near his feet. I felt woozy, my head fogging, and my eyelids drooping. The last thing I saw before I dropped off into a deep sleep were the Señor's eyes gazing into my own face. I felt very warm, very secure, and I heard his *meow*-voice assure me that everything was going to be okay. "Don't worry, Nobby," he said. "You'll love your new home."

Ever since that day, the Señor and I have had a marvelous time together. He told me that he was born in London, England. He traveled to Canada when he was a baby, and grew up in the city of Toronto. When he was only a boy, he learned to draw and paint, and also to play the violin. He loves

music. Often, early in the evenings, we sit together on the sofa and listen to classical music. It is very relaxing after a long day of painting. The Señor rises early. He sets up his easel in his studio or out in the garden.

We have adventures together in his studio and his big house and his sprawling garden where there's a grassy lawn and a pond filled with goldfish and a jungle of green plants. There are many different plants that climb up the high walls and have blooms of purple, orange, red, and yellow. The Señor understands what a fine and noble cat I am. He knows I'm not just a plain old stray alley cat or a simple pusscat. He knows I'm a computer-age cat with a great provenance and a wondering imagination. He knows I'm filled with promise.

Now, here's my story. I will tell of my adventures and I will exaggerate only slightly from time to time. As you shall see, I am also a poet. I will intersperse bits of verse from time to time, just to keep you on your toes. I hope you find it interesting. "Meow, meow," my way of saying, "Thank you."

Anyone can cat-sing simple songs:

Happy birthday to you,
Happy birthday to you;
Happy birthday, dear Nobby,
Happy birthday to you.

Or:

Meow meow meow,
Meow meow meow,
Meow meow meow,
Meow meow meow.

Or play the same tune on the piano. You have to find the first note, then the next, and so on. In music, it would be written in notes. But I don't read music, so I have to search for the notes. Usually, if I find the first one, I can move on to the second, the third, and so on. It's a relatively simple task, once you get the hang of it.

There once was a famous composer who couldn't read music, nor could he write it down. He would have someone do it for him. His name was Irving Berlin. *Purr*haps, I tell myself, I could be the cat version of this great composer.

I like complicated melodies, like "Some Enchanted Evening," but they are very difficult to play. I know that "playing by ear" is fun, but it's rather difficult for me. When I put my head on the keyboard, it begins to hurt. My ear won't cooperate. I need my paws.

Sometimes I wish I could take real piano lessons and play properly, not having to depend on my ear. Ah, but that's for another day.

Once, when everyone was out of the house, I jumped up onto the piano. My paws hit the keys and made a sound. I walked to one side, hitting the black and white keys, and the sounds continued. I discovered that if I walked one way, the sounds were deep and low. If I walked the other, the sounds were high, like a chirping bird. So I pawed my way up and down the keyboard, listening as I moved. When I moved faster, the sounds were quick and sharp. Hearing the bounce of the tune, I danced from key to key. If I banged hard, the sound grew loud. If I touched softly, the sound lowered. Now and then, I used my tail like the Señor uses his thumb, but my tail wasn't strong enough to make the key go down. Even if I couldn't do everything the way he does, it was still fun. Now and then, when all of the people are gone, I like to practice. *Purr*haps in the near future I will surprise the Señor and play a song especially for him.

The other day, the piano had been left open, so I leaped onto the stool, then onto the keys, and began a dance I'd recently learned.

I heard the Señor from the kitchen. I'd forgotten he had not left to go to town with the others. "Who is that playing the piano?" he called out.

I jumped down and quickly curled up on the sofa.

When he came into the *sala*, he said, "It must have come from outside or the TV upstairs," and went out again.

I opened my eyes, purred to myself, and meowed some nice melodies I'd like to play. *Purr*haps, if I can get someone to be my transposer, like Irving Berlin, I will compose a few tunes. And if the Señor likes them, he will send them off to his friends in Toronto, New York, or Los Angeles. I might even get them published and played on TV. If that happened, I'd be the first cat composer. Imagine that!

I might even teach my friend Florence to sing with my music. A beautiful cat, she has a sweet *meow*-voice. If she got an audition, I'm sure she would be a hit with a microphone. In my imagination, I can see her on the stage of a nightclub or in front of the lights on a television show. As they say, she'd be a natural.

But nowadays, playing music isn't absolutely necessary. They have synthesizers, I'm told, that make harmonies and chords automatically. All you have to do is push one note, and off it goes. Then, if you turn certain buttons, it will play sounds like a violin or a trumpet. If I got one of those for Christmas, I could be a one-cat orchestra.

Some musicians become quite famous by sitting at a piano and making no sounds at all for a half-hour. That's some people's idea of a concert. The audience just sits and watches and imagines their own sounds. When the musician pushes back his stool and stands and bows, the audience knows he's finished, and they applaud.

So, I ask myself, *why do I need to practice?* I will just stick with painting, where I'm already known for my talent. I can knock over one of the Señor's painting jugs, spilling colored water onto a canvas or a sheet of paper. I can step in some of his acrylic paint and dance across the canvas, making elaborate paw marks. Or I might even open a Catademy

and teach talented felines to do the same as I. I could even organize an exhibition and call it Paw Prints by Pusscats. You might find it soon on my new website: Art for All, The Nobby Catademy, Cat Paw meow meow dot com.

But here I go again. I put the wagon before the horse, as the old saying goes. My imagination is so active, I jumped ahead of myself. I'm so excited about telling my story, I want to tell it all right up front. I will try to tell it the way it happened.

BIRD WATCHERS

In my maturity, I have become a bird watcher. No longer a bird hunter. Like me, when I was younger, the Señor used to go bird hunting with his friends. They would awaken early in the morning and ride out into the *campo* and look for doves. Sometimes they would hunker down in marshes or undercover near the *lago* where they would wait for the unwary ducks or geese. Some geese flew all the way from Canada to escape the snow and icy weather of their homeland, trying to find warmth and peace in Mexico. Does it seem fair that hunters hide in the marshes, then surprise the birds with their cocked shotguns?

One morning the Señor came home after a hunt. He had three geese in his bag. He took them out one at a time, began pulling their feathers, preparing to make a meal. On the leg of one bird he found a band: "BIRD SANCTUARY—OHIO—UNITED STATES. PLEASE WRITE IF FOUND."

Reading the words, the Señor felt the weight of sorrow on his heart. Suddenly he wished he had not shot the peaceful bird that had innocently flown south. He put away his shotgun and vowed never to hunt again.

Now, when the geese fly overhead in a big **V** across the sky, the Señor takes his binoculars and watches. He listens as the geese honk their sounds. The sound makes him smile.

Sometimes I sit next to him in the garden as he watches all kinds of birds. He studies a book with pictures and names of various birds. When he sees a new bird, he looks it up in the book and writes

down the name. He is very meticulous in this new sport.

Also in the garden, swallows come and build mud nests under the eaves at the top of the walls outside the Señor's studio. When I see them, they make me wonder: *How do they find their way back to our garden every year?* In the summer, they fly north and disappear. In the winter, they come back. At the same time each year they find their way to San Miguel de Allende, up here in the mountains, in the center of Mexico. For five years they have done this. The Señor watches the baby birds break out of their tiny eggs, chirp, and beg for food. Then the mother feeds them. They grow feathers and flap their wings. Ultimately, the mother pushes them out to teach them to fly and they learn to find insects to feed themselves. The Señor says this is a cycle of nature.

In the late afternoons we watch the redheaded woodpecker chopping a hole in a tree, building a home for himself and his family. Mexicans call him *el carpintero*, the carpenter. We also find orioles with bright yellow vests, and hummingbirds that buzz around like overgrown bees, sucking nectar from the blossoms of the bougainvillea. There's a noisy black crow and black grackles that come and drink in the fountain. Sometimes they wait for the Señor to put out cat food. If the nuggets are too large and hard, the birds will dip them in the water to soften the texture, then peck the nuggets until they can swallow the remainder of the food.

I watch, because the Señor has made me aware of their beauty and interesting habits. When other cats try to catch the birds, I try to stop them, but I'm not always successful. *Purr*haps I will hold a seminar for the cats and teach them about the cycle of life and tell them about how smart some birds are.

Once, soon after I arrived at the *hacienda* in San Miguel, I caught a bird and took it to the Señor. I wanted him to know how much I appreciated his taking care of me and giving me a home. But the Señor yelled at me and took the bird out of my mouth. The bird flew away, leaving some feathers behind. The Señor scolded me in a harsh tone. I tucked my head, feeling badly. At that moment, I decided to stop being a hunter. I would dedicate myself to becoming a bird watcher.

Once I saw the big white *garza*, who looks like a stork. He flew in a circle overhead, then dove down and dipped into our fishpond and grabbed a goldfish and flew away with it dangling in his claws. I ran after him but couldn't catch him. If I see him again, I'll try to stop his evil ways. We love to watch the fish swim in the pond. They are harmless creatures that look pretty and swim in circles. Sometimes I sit next to the pond and watch them for hours. The Señor says they are soothing to watch, and I know he's absolutely right.

Copy Cats

Why do some people call other people "copy cats"? As far as I'm concerned, we don't go around copying things.

Why don't they say "copy dogs"?

I've been researching the subject. Flipping through some of the Señor's books, I find nothing in fables or classic stories about the beginning of "copy cat" as a slang phrase. If I knew any cats older and wiser than I, I would seek their advice. But there are no older or wiser cats. All of my friends are younger.

I know this: such a saying has to start somewhere. In English, people call a scoundrel or a trickster a "dirty dog" but you wouldn't call him a "dirty cat." That wouldn't make a lick of sense. Especially since cats are very clean. We're always washing ourselves and cleaning our fur. We are very tidy when we go to the bathroom. Because we cannot flush a toilet, we cover what we have done with earth or sand in the garden, or litter in the box.

We don't go around copying things, unless it is some important information I need to write about. As far as I know, nobody has ever copied me. *Purr*haps Whiskers will chase a ball if I'm chasing it too, but any other cat would do the same. Even so, she isn't a copy cat.

It would be wise of cats in the cat universe to copy me, since I am a special cat. Also, if they were smart, they would soon discover there is only one Sir Nobby, and that's me. If they try to copy me, they would only look ridiculous. *Hah!*

Of course, a person can be catty, if they are inclined to show such an attitude. If they wish, and if they are rich, they could be a "fat cat". There can be any number of other demeaning epithets that may fit a particular individual, but "dirty cat" is not one of them. Even the poorest of families don't have a dirty cat—although there is always Scruffy the Scrap Cat. But here I go again, putting a cat tale before its time. Hold on and I'll tell you about Scruffy in due time.

NOBBY'S ADVICE FOR CAT LOVERS

Cats are cats. They make up their own rules. If you realize that fact, life becomes easier for everyone.

Don't try to punish your cat. Don't roll up a newspaper and swat him. He's not a dog. Don't treat him like a dog. If you do, a cat will think you are playing with him and will swat you back with his paws. Try a little *meow*-talk: "No! Don't scratch the furniture," or "You can't go outside yet." He'll understand. Cats know much more than you might think, even if he doesn't show it or say "Yes, sir" right back.

Don't feed a cat too much. Many cats are greedy. If food is there, they'll eat it. Then they get too fat and sometimes cough up their food. Putting out a litter box is a good idea. Cats know instinctively what to do with litter. Still, let your cat out into the garden as often as possible—even if they won't come back when you call. A cat will come back when he wants to return. At that time, he'll meow to let you know. We are stubborn animals with minds of our own.

Don't expect all cats to be nice pusscats. Each is an individual—which you will discover soon enough. One may be shy. He may not wish to be stroked or petted. Another might jump into your lap and beg to be petted. Your cat will express his or her personality in his or her own way. Alas, it doesn't always happen—but you can try to make a friend. Be patient. Don't rush things. Sometimes, if you simply provide the necessities—food, water, and litter—and otherwise ignore your cat, he will soon jump onto the sofa next to you, rub his side against your arm, and purr happily when you stroke his coat. He might even lick your hand.

Don't be surprised if your cat becomes moody and turns away. If the weather changes suddenly, his mood changes, not unlike some people. Some cats become morose and sad when it rains. He may run for shelter and hide under a table or even a bed. He may stay hidden and listen to the downpour. I have known cats who like to get wet and enjoy a bath, but such creatures are very rare indeed. Most of us like to stay warm and dry.

I've heard people say you shouldn't get too fond of your cat. If you do, when they get lost or sick, it will upset you greatly. Well, if you ask me, that's a chance you will have to take. Love is a rewarding experience, I believe, and a cat will return your love and your care in his very own way. I don't have to explain this to true cat lovers; they know already and feel it in their hearts. There's an inner bond

we all have, even if we are only animals. It's a very special kind of feeling only a real cat lover knows—even if he or she doesn't quite know why.

If you find that you have adopted a computer-age cat, give him a chance and let him push your mouse around. He may want to go onto the Internet and even surprise you one day, asking if you will edit the manuscript of a book he's writing, like me. And if you've read this one, you won't be terribly surprised.

ACTING

"All the world's a stage and all the men and women merely players."

    A poet once wrote that line. I heard the Señor repeat it. Now its truth strikes me every day. When I'm out in the garden with Florence and Whiskers, I pretend I am someone else. I strut and fret, playing the part. But a cat is a cat. He can't change his looks and put on costumes the way people actors do. Still, I like to show off my talent for my friends. If they laugh, I'm successful. It's good to have a healthy laugh now and then.

    When I pretend to be someone else and walk out onto a stage and play-act the way some people do, my friends enjoy my antics. I'd like to dress up and become a cat-clown—with a funny hat and floppy clothes—or a soldier-cat with a sword and a fancy uniform.

    The best I can do is walk around differently. I can strut. I can wag my tail. I can scrunch down and slither across the floor. I can hide under the dining room table and pretend it's a forest where Robin Hood lives. I can even meow a sound that isn't my own meow, make a play-like growl of a mountain lion or a deep-throated purr like a pretty Persian.

    What the poet meant, I think, is that we change as time goes by. We become different every year, like when an actor changes his roles. For instance, I have been a kittycat, a pusscat, and a grown-up cat. Now I'm an old cat—or will be soon—and *purr*haps I will not be able to walk and will have to be put in a wheelchair. I might have to live in an old cat's home with other old cats. Then, when new

 young kittens are born, they will come out onto the stage the poet calls Life and begin the process all over again for a new generation. After all, that's what Life is all about.

I do more than jump up on things and scratch furniture to sharpen my claws. Last week, I did a very useful thing. I saved the house from being robbed by thieves.

The Señor had gone to a concert to hear some music in *el centro*. While he was gone, I lay curled in the bedroom, where he'd locked me. I was enjoying my nap when I heard a banging at the back door. Then I heard the sound of a crash somewhere in the house. Not moving, I heard strange voices in the hallway. As someone moved upstairs, the sounds became louder and louder. I was thinking about what I should do when the intruders began lifting the door from its hinges.

I dropped off the bed, crept toward the door, and scrunched down at the end of a bookcase. When three strange men entered, I slipped out behind them.

On my quiet cat's feet, I rushed down the stairs and waited.

As soon as the Señor came in, he saw me and wondered aloud how I could be here when he had locked me in the bedroom. He called the police, then hurried up the stairs.

When he came downstairs, the Señor was very happy. The burglars had had his violin and a prized box in their hands when they heard the Señor rushing up the stairs. They dropped the goods and fled. The police did not catch the burglars, but the Señor petted me and told me what a good cat I was. He said I'd foiled the burglary.

Ossito, the dog, had been in the garden when the strangers climbed the wall. But he is not a fierce guard dog. He's friendly to everyone. The burglars rubbed his head and gave him a bone, and he lapped their hands in his usual friendly way.

Every night I listen intently to the sounds outside. My ears are very sensitive. If I hear a strange sound, I awaken quickly and run to the Señor's bedroom, jump upon his bed to alert him. Sometimes he just pushes me away, thinking I want to play. But if I hear something that frightens me, I keep after him until he rises and goes downstairs. If he finds nothing, he says, "Oh, Nobby, what's wrong with you?" I can tell he's irritated, but I think it's best to be safe.

Whiskers

Within the soft paw
there is a sharp claw.
Just teach him
to use them,
but furniture—no!
So scold him
and teach him
and then let him go.
He might want
to use them
when chasing a ball
and finds them
most useful
when climbing a wall.

Nobby's Note: I take literary license now and then. I think an author has such a right. I asked Scruffy and some of the other animals to lend a helping hand with my memoirs. Now, here is a section or two provided by Scruffy.

SCRUFFY THE SCRAP CAT

Here I am—Scruffy. I am what my name suggests. I do my best with what I have. But what I have is not much. I'm a broken-down version of Sir Nobby, part Siamese and part alley cat. My fur is ragged and I can't keep very clean in this hole in the earth where I live. I don't have many cat friends. I catch birds and eat garbage scrap.

When I wander near their homes, other cats chase me away. Or they ignore me when they go out for a casual stroll. I watch that uptown cat, Sir Nobby, and I must say that I'm a bit jealous of his high-style breeding and his fine master and his beautiful home.

Once upon a time I lived high on the hill with a poor family. A boy with a face as dirty as my own scruffy coat put his stubby brown fingers on my back, and petted me gently. His sister, a little girl with long black hair, pulled my fur and told her *madre* that I tried to bite her. I don't know why she said such a thing. I wouldn't hurt anyone, much less a little girl.

When the mother shooed me away, I hid in the brush and waited until the boy was alone, then I sauntered out and approached him shyly.

When the boy bent to me and started to pick me up, the mother ran out of the little shack. She picked up a stick and threw it at me and told me to never come back.

I ran. Behind me, I heard the boy crying. I wanted to stop and go back to him and tell him everything was all right. But when I stopped, the mother threw a rock and hit me on the head.

I ran so hard and fast down the hill, I lost my footing. I tumbled claw over claw, falling into a briar patch, where I lay, breathing hard and hearing my heart beating loudly in my chest. Not moving, afraid that the mother had followed me down the hill with her rocks, I waited until nightfall.

In the dark, I pushed my way up. Briars scratched at my dirty coat. One tore at my left ear. Finally, I stumbled onto an unfamiliar road and made my way through a strange *barrio* where people shouted, threw bottles, and cried out obscenities. When a chair broke through a window, I managed to skitter out of the way. Two men followed a woman out of a swinging door. The men stumbled and grabbed at the woman, who twisted from their reach. All three cursed as I crawled into a dark alley, where I found refuge between two garbage cans.

I was so tired, I closed my eyes and fell onto the filthy ground. When I awakened I looked around at the soiled containers, rusted cans, dirty rags, and a discarded straw basket. I rummaged through the garbage cans and found two tiny slivers of old meat. I ate fast, happy to have something in my stomach, and then I began searching for a place where I could sleep safely.

I wandered up and down the hills until I found a ditch running next to two high walls. Near the top of the ditch I found a trickle of water. I lapped it, my parched throat thankful.

Under the thick coverage of shrubs and low-lying trees I found a hole wide enough and deep enough for me to stretch out and sleep.

Now, when the other cats chase me in the streets, I have a place to run and hide. The ditch is my home. No other respectable cat would ever come into my smelly ditch. Here, I live in solitude.

As I lay in my hole, I ask myself many questions. Why am I so unlucky? Where did I come from? Was my father or mother Siamese? Why can't I just be like other stray cats?

Nobby's Note: We will come back to Scruffy later. You will soon know why I give him space in my memoirs and you will see why he has become very special to me.

PHILOSOPHER CAT

I s there a word: *philosocat*? If not, we should put it in our own cat dictionary because that is what I am becoming: a philosopher cat. I take things for what they are: "Oh well, *meow*, it's like that and I can't change it." Or, if I'm ill, I say, "It's too bad, it can't be helped, I'll be better tomorrow." You see, I'm very optimistic. Or, an *optimisticat*. As you have already seen, I like to play with words; it makes me happy.

In spite of many terrible happenings, my mood today was *very* optimistic. A stray cat came by, got into the garden, sneaked onto the patio, and ate my plate of food. When I saw what he had done, I left in such a hurry that I knocked over a jug of flowers on the dining room table. It was a beautiful arrangement that I'm sure the Señor would have painted, but after my awkward maneuver, the vase was broken into a hundred pieces. Later, outside in the garden, a burr caught in my fur and I couldn't claw it out or chew it off. Whiskers jumped on me while I was sleeping. I was stung by a wasp, and the sting hurt for a long time. It seemed to not be my day, but you couldn't tell me—no, I just kept going. I thought I might play a little tune and maybe even dance a jig. But someone had shut the lid on the piano and I couldn't practice. *So what?* I asked myself. When all the bad things happen, I have a little talk with myself: *Just forget all the bad things and go on living.* I will not worry. Nor will I get depressed. I laughed aloud and meowed a *meow*-tune and I knew things would get better soon—and they always do.

When Whiskers caught her paw in the half-open door, it hurt badly. I thought she was going to cry all afternoon. I tried to tell her to look on the bright side, but she just looked at me like I was a goofy cat. She didn't listen. She crawled off and lay in the sun and closed her eyes. Now and then I'd hear her moan. I did a little dance, thinking I'd cheer her up. But she just looked at me askance and shook her head and closed her eyes again. Some day, when she grows up, she will learn to be a philosocat. Nowadays, she can't push her troubles aside. But she'll learn. When she does, she will live a happy life. All humans have to learn these lessons too, but I've noticed that some don't and they are miserable most of the time. They think too much.

I remember an old cat when I was only a kitten in Tampico. He told me: "Don't think too much. You will only get in trouble, if you do. And don't worry. Things will turn out for the best." Now I know he was a wise old cat. I'm glad I listened to him. Bad thoughts can make trouble worse. I try to cheer up a mournful person by doing some of my best tricks and *meow-* talk but, unless they let themselves relax, they don't understand what I'm up to with my antics.

Many animals are philosophical. Most dogs don't think too much. They just ramble around and do whatever they do, without thinking. Old Ossito was very ill in his last days with us. He just lay around and moped. I tried to cheer him up. When he was a young dog, he was a rounder. In his old age, I reminded him about the time when he was a youngster. He smiled when I told him these stories. He knew I was just trying to help, and we remained friends.

We cats talk among ourselves. If you listen carefully you can learn many words. In the same way, I've learned much English, listening carefully when the Señor and his friends talk their people-talk. To talk *meow*-talk, you must pay attention to how loud or soft we meow. Short and quick meows are very important. If I say softly, "*meow*," it means much more than quick, sharp "MEOW!" A baby makes sounds to express his feelings long before he can talk. Listen to the way a cat says, "*MEE*-ow" in the morning (he's saying "good morning") and you will soon begin to learn new words and meanings of *meow*-talk.

Of course, everyone knows the meaning of a soft "*purr-purr-purr.*" There goes a happy cat, as he settles down, snuggling in bed or sitting on a nice warm lap.

If you listen carefully to what I'm saying, you will learn that I am a computer-age cat. I do more than just use the old *meow*-talk to communicate my ideas, my thoughts, and my philosophy to other cats around the world and to the Señor and his guests who come to visit. Ours, you see, is a sophisticated household.

The Señor has done some drawings of me but hasn't really and truly captured my good looks. He does them mostly when I'm asleep and they don't show my stunning blue eyes. I've been told that my eyes are sexy, and for me that's a great turn-on. I ask myself: *Why be modest about something you know is true?* In my book, false modesty is a terrible trait. You won't find me belittling myself. I want you to know the truth, not simply a bunch of nonsense about how poor and pitiful I am. I've grown tired of reading memoirs in which the subject tells you how poor his mama was or how his father went out at night and got drunk and came home and beat up everybody in the family. In spite of such a horrible background, the main character grew up to be an upstanding person with wonderful talent. You won't hear all that garbage from Nobby. I was born with an outstanding pedigree and I've been very lucky throughout life.

And I'm smart, too. I like to read, as I am sure you have deducted from the style of my memoirs. I've been researching the history of cats and people. We go a long way back in time. Our association with people has been recorded for thousands of years. Long before Jesus Christ walked the earth, cats were worshipped in the courts of Kings and Shahs. Ladies in Middle Eastern harems kept cats as pets. Ladies put their precious jeweled rings on our tails for safekeeping. Did you know that Cleopatra owned a cat and thought the feline was the incarnation of royalty? It is absolutely true. She also put jewelry on her cat's tail. That's why many of us—especially the most regal ones, like me—still have knobs on our tails. After all, that's why the Señor named me Sir Nobby years ago.

Now, as I have reiterated a number of times to make a point, we live in the age of the computer. Computers have changed our world. It changed mine. As soon as I discovered the computer, I jumped up, took the mouse in my paw, and became fascinated when the screen came to life. It was better than flipping pages of the Señor's encyclopedia or dictionary. It took me places I'd never been and would never have seen, if it hadn't been for my agility with the mouse.

The first time I jumped up, hit the keyboard and grabbed the mouse, all I saw in front of me on the screen was confusion. Then I heard the Señor explaining how the mouse worked. As I tend to do, I watched and listened carefully. He said that all you had to do was push the little plastic mouse this way and that way, click it between your fingers, and all sorts of things would happen on the screen.

He wrote, or he drew, or he sent messages and letters, or he saw pictures of things happening on the other side of the globe. It was truly amazing!

I gave the situation much thought. I found my place on the back of the sofa, where I lay and watched, playing possum. I love to play possum, when the Señor thinks I'm napping but am actually just lying there with my eyes closed, thinking. *I can do that.* I watched his every move. *It's just a mouse,* I told myself. If anyone can do it, certainly an old veteran mouse-catcher like me can do it.

After the Señor left his chair, moving out to his studio to do some painting, I moved gingerly toward the computer. I jumped up onto the chair. I explored the keyboard and gazed into the blank screen. I flicked the mouse and touched a few buttons, then suddenly a bright blue color exploded on the screen. I almost broke and ran. But I didn't. I stared in amazement at the screen and its brilliant colors.

I touched another key and heard a *bong* sound from somewhere inside the machine. Then I saw a word on the screen—*e-letter*— and knew it was a message from someone for the Señor.

E-letter! The word echoed in my eyes. If other cats would make themselves computer-wise, I could communicate with my brothers and sisters around the world. I could do it. I knew I could. *Purr*haps I could create a *meow*-message on the computer and turn it into a cat-computer. As a wise and intelligent cat, I could place my name in nomination as president. Or I could form a company: Meow, meow—Feline dot com. *It's an idea*, I thought. Only an idea in the beginning, I would give it much thought and it might settle into something big and wonderful. Who knows? As always, my imagination whirred.

Opening the computer with a click of the mouse, I entered another world. My imagination knew no end. I moved from website to website. Here I was: Sir Nobby, starring himself. I sat at the computer for hours, a computer cat looking noble as an Egyptian statue. I dreamed of shifting my inner self through the screen into one of those elaborate sites, where you would be able to see me and hear me, and I would offer advice to forlorn felines around the world: *El Gato Nobby*, www.Nobbyland.com.

DRAWING

I t's easy to draw a sleeping cat. Be careful and don't disturb him. Don't make him stir and move.

As I sit before the computer, I have drawn Whiskers several times. I put her on skis in the Rocky Mountains. Then I shifted to the Caribbean and had her sailing on the beautiful blue-green water. If you have an active imagination, you can dream anything and go anywhere and do everything on the computer. Now I have to learn how to make a printout from the screen to the paper. I could probably even sell these cat prints, adding color to make them life-like.

Before I knew exactly what I was doing, I made a sketch of myself using the computer mouse. I pushed the mouse around. I drew a line that curled into a circle, then I connected the lines and brought them down. Try it! It's really easy!

Draw the ears separately, then the body, and then the legs and paws, attach the head and tail last.

Then put them all together.

Lastly, add eyes and whiskers. If you want a portrait, look at the nose and mouth.

Then the eyes.

And the whole face.

Now, fill in with a lot of shading here and there—and then—*presto!*—there it is.

El Payaso

I have heard it said that cats have no sense of humor. They don't smile and *meow*-talk with slaphappy funny jokes. They say dogs have a great sense of fun and will roll over when asked and some even manage what could be called a smile, when they're chasing a ball and bringing it back to their masters. However, all of this is *purr*fect nonsense. It is basic myth, *purr*petrated by people. We cats don't walk around with grins on our mugs. We don't tell *meow*-jokes understood by people. We won't fetch on command. But we have our own sense of humor, our own *meow*-jokes that are ours to understand and to keep to ourselves. Most cats are secretive. We have secrets we don't want every person to know and understand.

I've found an understanding of humor on the Internet that is *purr*haps lacking in the real world. One cat I know comes over to visit us in the garden. He will even eat a bite or two, when food is out. We call him *El Payaso*, Spanish for *clown*. He's a funny cat and he doesn't realize it. We like it when he visits, because something funny always happens to him. If he could wear clown makeup and baggy clothes, he could be a TV star. He would be a *purr*fect clown to work with a human straight man on a cat-*meow* program for a feline audience. They could make jokes, like "When is a cat not a cat?"

And the answer? Of course, "When he's dogging around," and *El Payaso* does a tumble and rolls over on his back and kicks his feet in the air.

El Payaso does other things too. He juggles balls. But he doesn't really juggle them, he tosses them into the air and bounces them off his head. He falls over things, jumps onto a table, misses, and lands on the floor. However, unlike most cats, he doesn't land on his feet. He proves all the old cliché beliefs about catdom wrong. He lands on his head. Then he gets up, shakes himself and *meow*-laughs, a sad kind of embarrassed *meow*-laugh, because we all saw him fall the wrong way for a cat. He looks up and out at his audience with big wide eyes, then he casts his look downward and gives a little shrug. We don't know what to do: laugh or cry. That's *El Payaso's* way of making his clumsiness funny. He's like Charlie Chaplin or Buster Keaton hanging from a flagpole in one of those old silent black-and-white movies. He's Charlie-cat or Buster-cat. His talent is enormous.

If he could be trained, like the lions who sit up on two legs or roll a barrel or jump through a hoop lined with burning paper, *El Payaso* would be a grand circus cat. But training a cat is very difficult, takes great patience, and deep understanding. For instance, I've never seen a cat retrieve anything for a master who throws a ball and asks the cat to bring it back. The cat will bring things to you, like the time I brought a bird to the Señor. We don't always obey orders; it's not in our nature to follow a leader, but we do answer when we're called to dinner, when we feel like it.

Whiskers is very obedient when she's called. Almost every time, she comes running. But she likes to tease, too. She will run to the door, then

refuse to go inside. She'll run away, chuckling to herself, saying she'll never be caught unless she wants to be caught. Although she says I'm sexist, I believe she's just being a typical female feline when she shows the Señor that she has her own way of doing things. I would never trick the Señor in such a sassy, saucy manner.

When I asked *El Payaso* where he lived, he said he and his mistress live alone in a house on the other side of our wall. They are very happy together. She even knitted a wool sweater for him for the winter, but he doesn't like to wear it and tries to tear it off when she pulls it over his head and pats it snugly to his body. He says it scratches and gets in the way of his legs when he needs to leap or run fast. When his mistress went away to Canada for two weeks, *El Payaso* was very lonesome. He didn't like the cat-sitter, who locked him in the house and was gone all day. He pined for his mistress and thought seriously about running away. One day, when he slipped past the cat-sitter and climbed our wall and lay with me in the sun in our garden, he told me his most secret thoughts. I told him that if he ran away he might never see his mistress again. And besides, if the old lady returned and found him missing, she would be very sad and even heartbroken. "Do you really think so?" he asked. I assured him that she loved him dearly. Why else would she spend all the time and energy to make him such a pretty wool sweater? He considered and finally decided it might be best to go home and wait for her to return. At least the sitter would have food out at the end of the day.

Several days later *El Payaso* returned to our garden and said he was even sadder than before. He did not look like a clown. He looked like a sad cat. We tried to cheer him up, but it seemed hopeless. I did a trick or two. I tossed a ball into the air, let it bounce against my head, and I fell over onto the grassy lawn. But when I looked, *El Payaso* stared open-eyed at me, his mouth turned down, his head resting on his paws. I tried again, but he didn't even smile. Whiskers nipped at his rear-end, and he growled half-heartedly, and she nipped again. He twisted his body around, playfully grabbing at her. I joined in the scuffle. *El Payaso* leaped onto the edge of the pond where the goldfish swam, then ran through the jungle of elephant-leaf plants. Whiskers and I followed, chasing him around a stone sculpture the Señor had placed next to the walkway. We ran and ran, until finally *El Payaso* collapsed on the grassy lawn, rolled over, and Whiskers touched his tummy with her paw. I sat nearby and suggested we have a bite of food. After *El Payaso* took several bites and lapped up some water, he said he had better return to the house. Even if he didn't like the sitter, he did not want to make her worry.

Several days later, *El Payaso* returned, saying he'd overheard the sitter on the telephone talking with his mistress from Toronto. The old lady would be returning in several days, and he wanted to surprise her with a gift. "Come with me," I suggested, and he followed me into the computer room, where I showed him how to use the mouse. After several short lessons, he was moving the mouse around the pad. He grinned at me, nodding happily as he followed my advice. Before we finished, he was doing some rather remarkable drawings of himself. One sketch showed him playing golf. I looked at it and laughed. Can you imagine a cat playing golf? Well, I can. But I can imagine almost anything. We printed his drawings. He took them home to surprise the old lady who loved him so much.

I have written a few lines of verse about our friend *Payaso*:

Our Friend, Payaso, the Clown
A smile on the face of this cat
Is not because he's smelled out a rat.
It's the food that he's eating,
It can never be beaten
And never will make him too fat.
Because he's our friend, El Payaso,
He's a super funny clown of a cat.

CATNAPPED

Not long ago, something happened that made me sick to the bottom of my stomach. Early one afternoon I decided to take a stroll through our part of town. I'd heard the Señor and several of his friends talking about how safe the streets of San Miguel are, especially during the daylight hours. I had heard hammering and sawing and the cheerful sounds of workers on the next block up the hillside, where they were building a new house. The Señor told his friend, the writer from the United States, that a family from Mexico City was building the house. I decided I would venture up the street and take a look for myself. *What would our new neighbors look like?* I wondered. I hoped the new neighbors might have a new cat, *purr*haps a purebred Persian female feline, or even a chocolate Siamese not unlike me.

During the first half-block beyond *el callejon*, beyond the drainage ditch that during dry season stank of soiled trash that settled there when the daily rains were not washing it from the poor homes high on the hill, I stayed in the shadows. When I saw the workmen perched high on a roof, laying orange tile that gleamed in the sunlight, I moved out of the shadows and worked my way toward the gate that opened into the space that would soon become a garden. Although it was now barren, I imagined how it might look with jacaranda, hyacinths, bougainvillea, and other colorful plants. With the multi-tiered fountain that now sat forlorn in the middle of the square yard, it would become a paradise for some lucky cat.

Heavy with my thoughts about what this *hacienda magnifico* would become in the near future, I sashayed onward, not thinking about security. I heard children playing, a sound that always calls me to discover new friends.

When I rounded a corner, I saw a dozen young boys running in different directions. One kicked a round ball, then the others chased after it. When one boy kicked the ball toward two wooden posts, another tried to catch it. When he missed, three girls standing next to the field jumped up and down, clapped wildly, and cheered the boy who had kicked the ball.

I found a place in the shade of a scrawny tree. I watched as the boys romped through the dust, now kicking the ball and chasing it toward the opposite end of the field.

All at once, while I was enjoying the sport, a rickety pickup truck screeched to a halt near me. A young man dressed in a T-shirt and blue jeans jumped out of the front seat of the truck. He ran over and grabbed me before I could leap away. I tried to scratch, but he had a strong hold on me. Then he gripped the loose skin behind my neck. Before I knew it, he shoved me into a metal cage in the bed of the truck. I gave a catty-whomp scream, hoping someone would hear my call for help. I heard the little girls cry out, but they were only cheering the boys on the playing field.

The man who'd grabbed me jumped into the cab of the truck, slammed the door, and the driver took off down the road.

I was so scared I didn't know what to do. I had no idea where they were taking me. I looked out the top of the wire cage, trying to spot something I could identify from my previous jaunts outside the Señor's compound. But I recognized very little. Once the Señor, when he took me to the veterinarian, let me look out the window of his van. We passed a thickly wooded park and several beautiful haciendas the Señor said had once been the homes of a movie star and an opera singer, then we bounced down a narrow cobblestone street, and pulled through a high gate into a paved patio.

But nothing I saw out of the top of the truck reminded me of any of previous trips. I saw wires running from high poles to tops of houses. When we passed one tall house, I saw a ferocious-looking dog pacing. I meowed loudly, trying to get his attention, but all he did was bare his teeth and continue to pace.

The truck pulled into a compound. I heard gates slam shut behind us. The man who had snatched me lifted the cage and jerked it out of the bed of the truck. He carried me to a concrete-covered patio

and let the cage drop to the hard surface. I lost my footing, slammed against the side of the cage, then found my balance and searched my surroundings. It must have been some kind of garage. I smelled motor oil and old grease. Somewhere in the distance I heard other cats meowing. They didn't sound friendly.

I hushed and listened. The other cats all meowed at the same time. I could not determine where they were located. Their sounds all blended together. Not like in a song. It wasn't happy. It was more chaotic than anything. They sounded afraid and disturbed, angry and alarmed. Soon, I realized, I felt the same emotions.

As I hunkered down and tried to think about what to do, I thought about the Señor. I had put myself in danger by wandering too far away from him. He would have no idea what had happened to me or where I was. For all he knew, I had run away.

He was probably disturbed and angry with me. He was probably cursing his stupid cat whom he'd always treated with great comfort and care. He loved me, and I repaid him by going too far away from him.

Suddenly, I shivered and felt terribly alone. I huddled in a corner of the cage, pushing my fur against the wires that seemed to be the bars of a prison. I would perish here. I knew I would. *Oh, Señor, please forgive me for my foolishness. Please love me and come looking for me. Please!*

SCRUFFY THE SCRAP CAT II

I was lolled out, sunning myself on the edge of a soccer field, watching the neighborhood children kicking their ball and running after it. Watching them, I thought it was a funny thing how boys, girls, and dogs chase balls. Seldom do you ever find a cat chasing a ball. A cat might slap at a ball of yarn or a rubber ball on a string. But don't throw a ball and expect a cat to run after it and bring it back to you.

I had just yawned and was about to close my eyes and take a nap when I saw a man in a rattletrap old pickup truck bounce over the rocks on the far side of the field. A fancy-dan chocolate Siamese whom I had seen strutting and prancing in the safety of his master's fancy garden was standing in the shade minding his own business. A man who looked as scruffy as me jumped out of the truck and grabbed the snooty cat before he had a chance to run away. The guy pushed the cat into a wire cage and threw it into the back of his truck. Then he slid onto the front seat and the driver sped away.

I stood immediately and took off after the truck. I had to run across the field and dodge between two of the soccer players. I ran so fast my paws barely touched the ground. Down the hill, where the truck's wheels kicked up dust, I saw it turn north and head down Prolongacion Aldama toward Juarez Park. I took a shortcut between two shanty houses and across the drainage ditch where I lived in a hole in the underbrush. When I came out on Aldama, I saw two children playing with their mutt-dog. I didn't like the dog. He was dirtier than me. He lived in an apartment over a *tienda* with

the family. As I sped by, the dog wagged his tail and barked. But I didn't have time to fool with him today—to fight or play. I continued in hot pursuit.

At the corner where the water fountain flowed, where I could sneak a drink in the hottest days of April or May before the rainy season started, the truck turned west through a narrow *callejon*. After a short block, it turned up another cobblestone street.

As I made the turn on two paws, almost toppling, I saw the truck disappear into a place where I had seen men working on automobiles and a motorcycle. Moments later, someone closed the gates behind the truck.

I drew to a halt at the bottom of the hill and eased over into the shade of a scrawny laurel tree. I scrunched down and breathed deeply. Although I have lived in and around San Miguel all of my life, when I run too fast, too long, I get short-winded. The high altitude gets to everyone eventually, even old veterans like me.

Resting on my haunches, I explored the territory. The patio of the garage was behind high walls. On this side was a three-story hacienda. Once upon a time, years ago, I spotted a high-toned white Persian stretched out on a colorful lounge chair next to a long mirror-slick pool in the garden of this house. I often wondered about the beauty of that sleek little Persian. She had regarded me with an upturned nose and a slight nod. I knew better than to try and make her acquaintance. An old reprobate like me didn't stand a chance with a lady like her.

Now here I was, thinking of ways to make myself a hero, when the thought of that afternoon's vision came to mind. I couldn't help but wonder what she might think if she knew about my planned heroics. Would she think about me differently? I shrugged. I doubted it.

Anyway, I wasn't standing out here on this dusty sidewalk, planning to help another haughty cat, because I wanted to look good in a lady's eye. I was doing it to help a fellow feline, and that was the simple fact of the matter. It is the thing you do, when you see an evil deed being done. Those scruffy-looking men in the pickup truck had stolen a cat. Now, I would do everything in my power to set the cat free. It was my duty.

I paraded past the gates and looked over the area. At a dwelling on the far side of the garage, a heavy, sturdy vine grew up a high wall next to the sidewalk. If I climbed up there . . .

I didn't think about it for even a rat's second. I grasped the vine in my claws, lifted my tail, and began my ascent up to where I could peer down and find out exactly where the hostage cat was being kept.

With each pull, I felt vulnerable. Glancing down, I saw the sidewalk far, far below. If I lost my footing, I'd make a cat-jump to land on my paws. But it would still hurt, when I hit the broken concrete of the old sidewalk.

Nevertheless, I kept pulling myself higher and higher, until I had a front paw over the edge. Then I pulled my body up onto the foot-wide ledge.

In the distance, I heard the distressful meows of the captured cat. The very sound of it made my heart flutter beneath my fur.

Why were some humans so awfully cruel to animals? I asked myself. Especially when the critters would do the humans no harm. *They just did these things for pure meanness*, I told myself.

After I worked my way along the high wall, I looked down onto a slanting tile roof that extended toward the open patio where I'd seen the truck disappear. I stepped gingerly down, my paw-claws barely touching the hard surface. I let my body drop, scrunching down, trying to be careful not to make a noise to alert the kidnappers. I felt like a circus performer on a highwire, balancing from step to step.

Just as I hit the halfway point, something happened. My paws slid against the surface. I reached out with my front right leg to steady myself, but my body fell in the opposite direction. I rolled over, reaching out with front and hind legs, but my paws slid across the roof and my body began to tumble.

I had to lean to the left for a true cat-fall. No sooner than my feet touched a bush, my body rolled into the branches. Something tore at my side. A sudden pain shot through my midsection.

I worked my legs as fast as I could. Freeing myself from the branches and thorns, I scampered wildly across the pavement.

Hearing the commotion, the man who had handled the cat cage ran out of the garage and headed toward me with a broom. He swatted in my direction, but I skittered away from him, spotting another bank of flowering vines. I leaped, grabbed one of the larger vines in my claws and jimmyed myself up and out of his reach.

"Get out of here, you mangy animal!"

I climbed to the top of a higher roof and pulled myself over another ledge, onto a patio on the second floor. I hid behind a large flowerpot and breathed deeply. My lungs were sore as I heaved in and out, in and out, gulping air.

Momentarily, I moved through an open doorway into a strange bedroom. I listened intently. Hearing no sound, I got down as low as possible and crawled under the bed.

I closed my eyes, continuing to breathe deeply. I was so tired, in spite of my anxiety I soon dropped into a deep sleep. When I awoke, I was surrounded by darkness. It took me a moment to realize where I was. Again, I listened intently. Hearing no sound, I crawled out and gazed around the dark room.

The door I'd entered was now closed. Panicked, I darted around the room. My heart sank. *Did they know I was here?* Surely not, I decided. If they knew I was here, I too would have been locked in a cage.

Somehow, I knew I wasn't in danger of being catnapped. The scruffy man clearly didn't like my looks. All he did was try and chase me away. He knew no one would pay a ransom for my return. I imagined he'd already contacted that snooty Siamese cat's owner and asked for a reward. That's the way some crooks operate in this world. They find a helpless cat who has wandered away from his home, grab him, lock him up, then ask for a reward.

What am I doing here? I asked myself. *Would the Siamese do it for me?* I doubted that he would. Still, beneath my matted, filthy coat, I did have a sense of honor. After all, a cat's a cat, for all of that.

After surveying my options, I decided to return to my warm place under the bed. I sprawled out and shut my eyes and drifted into a delightful dream about piles of good cat food and an ocean of good, cool, clear water.

Either late at night or early in the morning, I heard voices in the hallway outside the bedroom. As the voices got closer, I crawled to the edge of the bed and peeped out just as the door opened and someone came into the room. From my place, I saw only the shoes: men's high-top work boots.

I slid from beneath the bed. Lucky for me, the man had left the door cracked. I slithered around it, careful to make no noise. I was down the stairs before you could say "General Santa Ana." I moved through the dining room, where shadows from outdoor lights made the table and chairs appear gigantic.

In the kitchen, I found a window open. I leaped onto the cabinet, climbed over a pile of dishes in the sink, and started to jump.

A dish slipped beneath me and fell to the floor, crashing.

I didn't wait to see if I had awakened anyone. I sped through the window and jumped onto a tall evergreen bush and slid down its side. The cedar spines cut into my paws, but I didn't slow down.

Amid outside shadows, I searched the smelly patio.

I meowed softly, hoping the Siamese would hear me. I just hoped he would not screech loudly, which might alert the man upstairs.

As I rounded a corner to look into an alcove, I heard a soft *meow*.

I stopped and waited, listening.

Another soft *meow*. The sound was barely audible.

It came from behind a high heavy door. I raised up on my hind legs and pushed at the door, but it wouldn't budge.

I looked around and spotted a large chest filled with tools. But such tools are useless in a cat's paws.

Nearby was a hoe, leaning against a wall. I pushed against it until it fell in the direction of the door. Then I worked my shoulder under the blade until it rose to meet the door handle.

On the third try, the blade caught on the latch. I let it fall. The latch snapped and the door creaked open just wide enough for my body.

I rushed into the room, where the cage holding the Siamese sat in a corner.

A higher-pitched *meow* came from the cage.

I meowed back, telling him not to worry.

With his nose, he showed me the clasp on the high corner. I worked a paw beneath the clasp and lifted.

At first it wouldn't move.

I pushed my paw harder, using all of my strength.

The clasp moved slightly.

Then I twisted.

CATNAPPED II

I was so glad to see the ugly cat. He looked beautiful to me. As he entered the room where I was being held captive, I meowed my welcome.

When he got close to the cage, I saw that his front leg had been injured. He wasn't bleeding but the fur above his paw had been torn. A big chunk of fur had been ripped from his side.

As wounded as he was, he didn't hesitate to put his paw under the latch and lift. I could tell from his meow that he was in pain. Still, he pushed hard, and on the third attempt, with my help, the top of the cage popped up and open.

I scrambled out and followed the cat to the door.

"Let me help you," I offered, but he only shrugged and told me not to bother.

"Follow me," he said, and led the way through the open patio to a wall of flowering vines. He began to climb slowly upward. About five feet above the floor, his grip slipped and he fell back. I held fast with my left paw and reached out with my right to steady him. He fastened his claws onto a vine and pulled himself up, grunting.

"Don't try to go so fast," I said.

"We've got to get out of here," he said. He pulled up and away from me. I followed.

At the top of the wall, he reached down with his good paw and gave me a final jerk.

On the roof, we cat-walked around two corners, found a back staircase, and tiptoed down to street level. Outside, he told me his name was Scruffy and pointed the way down a steep hillside. Together, we made our way through an alleyway. At a public fountain we stopped and lapped up some water. I was very thirsty, but Scruffy warned me not to drink too much too fast. Then we proceeded up *Prolongacion Aldama* to *Calle de la Quinta*, where we turned to head toward the Señor's house.

Outside the hacienda, Scruffy said, "This is where we part ways."

"No, no," I insisted. "Come with me and let the Señor feed you and fix your sore leg."

Scruffy was hesitant. "He'll only chase me away," he said.

"Not when I tell him about how brave you are—that you saved my life," I said.

I scratched at the door and meowed loudly.

In a few minutes, Alfredo, who lives in the adjoining *casita* and helps the Señor with the upkeep of the garden, pushed open the door.

I walked down the pathway toward the garden. I meowed for Scruffy to follow. When he limped after me, Alfredo shouted for him to stop. I meowed loudly, went to Scruffy and motioned for him to come with me. Alfredo backed away, watching us enter.

At the glass door between the *sala* and the *jardin*, I again scratched and meowed with a certain urgency.

Momentarily, the Señor opened the door and proclaimed, "Nobby! Where have you been? I've been so worried. And you brought a friend?"

I nodded and pushed my shoulder against Scruffy's side and pointed my paw toward his injured side.

"My, my, old boy, what's happened to you?"

The Señor bent down and touched Scruffy's side.

Scruffy winced and meowed hurtfully.

"Just a minute, and I'll fix you up," he said, and went back inside. A little while later he reappeared with a bowl piled high with fresh food and some bandages. He applied an ointment to Scruffy's leg while he gobbled up the food.

Poor old Scruffy looked like he was starving to death. He ate so fast, some of the nibbles caught in his throat and he had to cough.

"Take it easy, old fellow," the Señor said. "You don't have to rush."

The Señor seemed to know that Scruffy had saved me. He said that a man had approached him, saying he'd found a cat that looked like his Sir Nobby. But the people who had me, the man said, wanted a handsome reward for my return.

"The first thing on my schedule this morning was to go to the bank and cash a check," he said.

I meowed softly and rubbed next to the Señor's leg. He reached down and petted me. "We'll have to make your new friend welcome," he said. He went back inside, found an

old blanket, and put it next to my outside bed on the portico. "Whenever you want in, either follow Nobby or scratch on the door yourself."

As Scruffy curled up on the old blanket, he had a smile on his face.

It was not until then that I recognized him as the thief who'd come over the wall and had eaten my food. Alfredo had said he was a bad cat and I had agreed. Now, I knew better. He was my friend who had risked his life to save me.

Later in the day, we learned from the Señor that there were bad people in some of the *barrios* of San Miguel who earned a living by kidnapping cats and dogs. They would grab them on the street, just like the man snatched me. When the pets' owners posted rewards on walls or telephone poles, the kidnapper would call, say he'd found the cat or dog, then return the animal and collect the money. Then he would go back out and snatch another pet.

Back when I lived near Tampico, my masters lost their favorite poodle when he went out onto the street by himself. They offered a reward, but no one ever came to collect. They were very sad and missed the little yapping dog. But I didn't miss him, and I imagine that is why they gave me away to the Señor. They saw I had no remorse about the missing dog. I was selfish and not very nice. But I was younger then. Now I've matured into a more caring animal. I am wiser and more lovable. I care for my new friend Scruffy. While I am still the dignified Sir Nobby, I guard over my injured friend and will make sure he recovers sufficiently.

After his nap, I told him about my noble ancestry and how I have become a world-famous cat known as Sir Nobby. He listened with half-open eyes, nodded, and did not comment.

Nobby's Note: Now you know why I give special favor to my friend Scruffy, allowing him to write in my memoirs. And now I will pay homage to him in my own words . . .

Scruffy the Great

I t's funny how our attitudes change about people and cats. Once upon a time, I would have chased Scruffy out of our garden with a *fur*-ocious growl. I would sneak up on him when he'd come prowling through the underbrush to creep up on our food bowls. He would be getting ready to take a big bite when I'd jump out from my hiding place, frighten him, and chase him away.

Now, he's my hero. Scruffy still looks as though he just crawled out of a gutter, but I know deep down that he has a heart of gold. It all goes to show that you really can't tell a book by its cover, as the humans say.

I do everything I can to help Scruffy. I've tried to tell him he's welcome in our garden any time he wishes. The Señor has made the same overtures, not to use my own vast knowledge of language and music. If Scruffy could hear me, he'd say I'm showing off—and he's probably right.

Nevertheless, the other day I came upon Scruffy scribbling in the sand. "What are you doing?" I asked, eager to know what was on his mind. He tucked his chin and shook his head. "Nothing," he said shyly. I did not believe him. I had been talking with him recently and had told him I was writing my memoirs. I even suggested he would be the subject of at least several short chapters. He tried to act like he wasn't flattered, but I told him that he had become very important in my life. "I just did what came naturally," he said, trying to downplay his heroism.

"Now, what is it that you're hiding?" I asked.

Scruffy moved aside and let me read his scroll in the dirt.

As I read, I became quite moved:

I'm Scruffy, the scoundrely cat.
If you came here to find me
you'll not know where I'm at.
I hide in the daytime
and come out at night.
I scowl and meow, or I fight.
I look like a rascal
but I'm not really bad.
It's not easy to be loving
with the life that I've had.

I was so moved I asked if I could have his permission to use his verse in my memoir, and, after some strong *purr*suasion, he meowed his okay. After all, he's no longer as scruffy as his name suggests. He has cleaned up pretty well for an alley cat. Now he's a poet and he knows it. He's my friend. Wherever I go, he can go. One day I will teach him how to use the mouse and we will travel together across the Internet. And some day, if he continues to learn, he might even become Sir Scruffy.

INSTINCTS

L ike people, all animals have dreams. I have seen Ossito and other dogs bark and kick their legs as if they were jumping, though they were fast asleep. My guess is: they were dreaming of chasing cats or of being given a big bone for dessert.

Sometimes, I wonder if snails have dreams. Can you imagine a little snail having a dream about crawling along the surface of a green-leafed plant and leaving his shiny calling card?

Or what about a mouse? He would be dreaming about finding a big fat piece of Swiss cheese in a dark corner where he could chow down without being caught by a cat like me.

My dreams lately have been about a strange other world. It's a world I have never known. *Purr*haps my great ancestors passed these dreams down to me. Do you ever dream about camel races or riding atop a huge elephant's head, rocking to and fro? I've never done such a thing, but after sneaking in the back gate of a circus, when the Señor went to the soccer field where I was catnapped, I saw it happening and dreamed about it that night. That's the way my imagination works: I see something on TV or some strange happening, like the circus, then I begin to put myself into the picture. It's strange, but also wonderful.

Last night I pictured myself sitting on a golden couch, soft as a cloud. I leaned back, surrounded by beautiful, dusky harem girls who petted me and gave me bits of salmon and chunks of chicken. As they stroked my fur, I purred and purred. I let the goodies melt down my throat while I settled down and

watched some dancing girls. To my left was my new friend, Scruffy, but he was not scruffy at all. He was *purr*fectly groomed and enjoyed the vision as much as I.

Once I dreamed we had white rats as pets (*ugh*!). I let them out of their cages and they ran around me, doing tricks, entertaining me. Of course, I have never seen a white rat, but my imagination works wonders sometimes. That's what your imagination is all about: making an impossible world possible.

At times I have had bad dreams. Once, in a nightmare, I got caught in a rabbit snare that held me captive. It was worse than the catnapper's cage. Even though I've never been caught in a rabbit snare, the nightmare seemed *purr*fectly real; I awakened, kicking and flailing about. I looked around and saw Whiskers sleeping and felt immediately safe, warm and secure.

My most favorite dreams are when I'm eating something good or just snoozing on the back stoop, seeing a beautiful sunset at the end of a wonderful afternoon.

When cats go round and around, beating down the bedclothes with our paws, we are following our ancient instincts. We are pushing down the reeds and plants to make ourselves a snug and cozy bed. It's the motion our ancestors made, years ago. The great lions and tigers of Africa follow the same instinct in the wild. Now and then we revert from being nice tame animals to being wild once again, following our natural instincts.

A Wanderer

Sometimes I don't learn my lesson the way I should. I'm a wanderer by nature. I have a cat's instinct to look beyond the wall next door, over the hill, and around the corner. It wasn't long after the catnapping that I wandered up the hill again. Scruffy had gone back to his old home in the ravine near our house. Although the Señor told him it would fine for him to stay and live with us, I think Scruffy likes his old dirty hole in the ground. It's where he feels at home. He will return soon and stay with us for a while, then he will slip off into the night to find whatever appeals to him in the brush. When I crawled through a hole in our wall, I guess I was thinking that I was just as good as Scruffy—just as wild and rambunctious. I would show him that I too could go out into the world on my own, and I wouldn't get into trouble—even without my collar, which slid from my neck and over my head while I was crawling through the tight space.

While I was wandering, I managed to keep out of sight of the cat and dog police. I found a quiet place under some bushes to spend the day. I didn't bother to look for food. I could always go home. But I found some water in a street pool. Night came and I slept under a bridge. There were several stray cats who appeared to be at home in that dark place. I looked for Scruffy, but he was not among them. I spent the night under the bridge, but I didn't feel comfortable enough to actually sleep. When dawn came, I made my way back up to the street and began to search for my safe and lovely home.

Using my fine sense of smell, I retraced the last streets down which I had wandered. I kept thinking I would find my wall and the hole through which I had crawled when making my way out into the world. I looked and looked, but I could not find the wall.

As I went down a street that seemed familiar, I spotted the neighbor's maid, Marciana, and she saw me. "Nobby," she uttered. I threw back my noble head and yawled loudly, trying to let her know I was in trouble.

She crouched down and picked me up and put me into her shopping bag. At first, terror shivered through my body. Would Marciana catnap me? Would she try to collect a reward? I didn't think she would do something like that, but sometimes you never know.

I tried to calm myself. I meowed softly. I wanted to let her know that I was putting all of my trust in her.

Marciana reached down into the bag and stroked my head. "Don't worry, Sir Nobby," she said.

I breathed deeply, relaxing.

Some minutes later she knocked on the gate and Alfredo opened it and let her in. The Señor came into the garden and took me into his arms and petted me profusely. "I don't know what I'm going to do with you, old boy," he said. "I found your collar next to the wall. I didn't know what had happened to you."

I meowed to let him know he didn't have to worry. I would stay here and rub against his pant's leg. I would crawl onto the couch and snuggle next to him.

I was so glad I had made it through another bout of trouble without becoming an alley cat or without being taken to the cat shelter. And, heaven forbid, I didn't want to become someone else's pet. I was lucky. I had the Señor, who had alerted the neighbors to be on the lookout for me. He said they were very worried. They were afraid I might have gone off with Scruffy.

When Scruffy returned several days later, I told him about my adventure. He shook his head and meowed a warning. "You are a great, noble creature, Sir Nobby. You don't belong on the streets. You need the care of a terrific owner. You should remember that."

"Oh, quit preaching!" I told him. But I knew he was right. Down deep I enjoy being the object of the Señor's love and admiration. I know he cares, and that alone makes me feel really, really good.

HALLOWEEN

I'm sure you've heard people say, "Curiosity killed the cat." Well, I think it's partly true. We cats want to know what's happening. After all, that's what my careless wandering is all about: trying to find out what's around the next corner or over the next hill.

Last Halloween, I was very curious. The day itself has always fascinated me. It's one of my favorite times, when the witches come out and the ghosts haunt the streets and the gardens. Legend makes us a part of it as well—especially black cats, who are considered witchy and bad luck, which is not true at all.

Last Halloween, I checked up on what I thought I'd seen the year before—a group of witches taking off from a midnight meeting at the far end of our garden. I was thinking that *purr*haps they would come again this year. I was very curious to discover how their broomsticks work. Can they really just sit comfortably on a broomstick pole and fly about like an airplane? Once I tried sitting on our cornstalk broom but it wouldn't move an inch. I gave it my deepest concentration, but nothing happened. I also tried it on a garden broom made of twigs wrapped together, but still nothing happened. I closed my eyes and willed it to move and even made up a few words of magic, mumbling, "Move broom! Move across the room!" I even made some paw passes, thinking my touch would do the trick, but it still did not move.

On Halloween night, I made myself up to prepare for their arrival.

I put on a costume so I could creep up on them and sit nearby and not be spotted as an intruder. With a black cloak and a tall dunce hat, I was disguised *purr*fectly for their meeting. In this fashion, I'd just be another goblin out for a good scary night. Even if they spotted me, they would surely think I was one of them. I'd sit in the darkness, away from the light of their fire, and observe their witchery.

Scrunched down in the bushes near the place where they met last year, I watched and waited. At the stroke of twelve, I heard a swishy sound overhead. I craned my neck and looked into the night. Then another similar sound  swished nearby. It was so eerie it made me shiver. In the light of the full moon, I saw first one, two, then more. They flew in from all directions, each sitting on her broom as easily as the teenager on the hillside rides his motorcycle. They glided about in a circle. One carried a smoky pot hanging from her stick. Another held a handful of matches. Soon they landed and sat in a circle. They stacked sticks together. A fire was lighted. The pot was balanced over the blaze. One poured water into the pot. As it continued to smoke, another shook salt and pepper into the brew.

Suddenly it crossed my mind that they might be preparing something terrible, something evil. *What if . . .*

Something unthinkable wiggled through my brain, but I pushed it away. I looked across the garden toward the fish pond and the patio. The house was very dark. There was no sign of life anywhere. No one stirred. Not even Whiskers or Scruffy.

I couldn't back down now. Not even if I wanted to. I hunkered down closer to the ground, hoping the bush would keep me hidden.

Where had they come from? Why were they here?

I couldn't understand a word they were saying. Their voices screeched, cracked, crackled, making weird, frightening sounds. Theirs were crazy words, like English spoken upside-down or Spanish sounding sideways, all broken into gobble-de-gook, things like "Blig, swishly, snaggle" and "Trelly smig smushy smook." Now and then they would make a laughing sound.

I studied their brooms. They looked like the ordinary kitchen variety. I saw no miniature motors or wings or foot-pedals. Nor was there a seat or a backrest. No fancy late models with frills.

Then one witch raised her scrawny, clawed finger, and everyone fell silent.

Had they noticed me?

I prepared to ditch my hat and cloak and run as fast as I could. Maybe I'd leap onto the vines and climb over the fence. *Purr*haps I would find Scruffy's hole and hide in it.

Then the witch dropped her hand, like a sign. Her fingers wiggled up and down. The others hushed.

As I watched them, my heart beat heavy in my chest. Although I wanted to wait long enough to discover what they might put into the steaming pot, I became afraid that they might have noticed me. I knew I didn't want to be made into a witch's stew.

I began backing out from beneath the bush. I pawed silently away, keeping my head down and my chest near the ground. I stole away without waiting to watch them mount their brooms and wave goodbye.

Where they went, I do not know. *Purr*haps they are now meeting in *your* garden. If you go softly into midnight some Halloween night, *purr*haps you can catch them boiling up a brew. But if you do, make sure you are disguised *purr*fectly for such a meeting. Or *purr*haps by now you've learned how to fly on your very own broom.

Have you had dreams that seemed so real you were frightened afterwards? One night I watched Ossito sleeping. He was growl-mumbling at another dog or someone, and when he woke he knew he'd been living a frightening experience. Still later, he couldn't believe what he'd seen and done was not real. That's what happened to me. I had been looking at TV witches and ghosts and seeing them come to our door, little witches and goblins, singing out "trick or treat?" and looking so real that I believed I had slipped out into the garden at midnight on Halloween and eavesdropped on the witches making their brew. My imagination worked its tricks, giving my dream a reality that still makes me shiver. The next morning, I even went out into the garden to look for the embers of their fire and to see if they left behind part of a broom or one of their pointed hats. But I found no sign of them anywhere.

Back inside, I found the computer unmanned. I jumped up and touched the mouse with my paw and went online. In a *purr*fect moment, I sent a message.

Wanted: Witches Broomsticks.
Any condition—flyable, modern, or antique. Used witch hats would be appreciated.
Please contact: brooms-witches dot com.

Now I'll await my answers.

A CHRISTMAS CATASTROPHE

We all have fun at Christmastime. In early December the Señor gathers fluffy green branches from trees in the garden. Then everyone puts the branches together to make a Christmas tree on a table in the living room. Whiskers and Scruffy and I watch while the Señor, Alfredo, and some of their friends begin to decorate. They put on red and green lights that twinkle on and off, string a festoon of gold and silver streamers around and around, and hang colorful balls and silver stars. Then they stack boxes of presents under the tree and wait for Christmas morning.

The tree was especially pretty this Christmas. On Christmas Eve everyone admired it and talked about how wonderful it was. While Scruffy napped on the portico, Whiskers and I watched the last of the presents being laid beneath the tree.

After the Señor made the final toast, saying how much Santa would love this tree, Whiskers and I curled up on the sofa. Long after I heard the Señor's footfalls descend up the stairs, I heard a banging noise.

The crash was loud enough to awaken me, but I didn't budge from my warm spot. I opened my eyes and peered through the darkness.

The red and green lights were no longer strung high on the tree. They twinkled in a clutter on the top of the table. The streamers no longer glittered in their rhythmical pattern. They lay in a heap in the darkness.

An awkward scratching came from the middle of the debris. Then I knew what had happened. Whiskers, who was always curious and clawing at things, couldn't resist the temptation. Seeing a silver star swinging in the magical lights, she reached up and swung. When she did, her paw hit a limb and tore it loose. After that, it was like a house of cards; it tumbled down into a heap on top of Whiskers.

After I determined my cat-friend was not injured but suffered only hurt feelings, I closed my eyes and dreamed about Santa Claus bringing a big sack of catnip.

At first light, I was awakened when the Señor declared, "What on earth! Who . . ."

Disappointment and dismay covered his face as he explored the wrecked tree, the pile of lights and decorations, the whole big mess. He shook his head.

His eyes glanced first in my direction, then he saw Whiskers with a silver star dangling from an ear and a frosty streamer hanging around her neck. "Whiskers!" he growled.

He stomped across the floor, opened the back door, and shooed both of us out of the house. Scruffy looked up from his bed of old blankets and didn't know what to think about the sudden turn of events. It was obvious that he too had been dreaming of Santa.

Through the back windows we watched as the Señor tried to put the tree back into order. He picked up branch after branch and fashioned them into shape, then placed the lights and the streamers. Then he backed away and gazed at his work.

But he didn't invite us back inside until much later, after friends stopped by and eggnog was made and presents were opened. We sat outside on our haunches and stared forlornly through the windows

at their merry-making. Finally, the Señor opened the door and said we could come inside, if we *all* behaved ourselves. As he spoke, he glared directly at Whiskers, who put her chin down against her chest and purred mournfully.

The Señor raised his glass and laughed and said, "Well, Merry Christmas to everyone."

At the dining table, he picked up a piece of turkey and handed it down to Whiskers, showing his forgiveness. "Peace on earth and good will to all men—and cats."

We all purred softly and felt better. After a little holiday cake, we were allowed to open our presents.

Eyeglasses

Have you ever seen a cat wearing eyeglasses? I have. One time I tried on a pair of the Señor's glasses, but I couldn't see through the lenses. I thought about going to a cat eye-doctor, or a cat-optometrist, but I decided that wasn't really necessary. My eyes don't go out of focus, like a dog's. Besides, animals would look rather funny going about with glasses perched on their heads.

This is how I looked:

Was I not cute?

Maybe the cat-optometrist could fit me with contact lenses, if I needed help. That way, I wouldn't look so funny and I could get used to wearing them.

However, if I could wear a monocle on one eye, it could be the trademark of the sophisticated Sir Nobby. I'd wear it cocked just so, or I could simply carry it on a cord to look impressive.

CATS & KITTENS

Since I put myself on a higher plane than most felines, becoming a birdwatcher and swearing that I would never ever harm another bird, I have had a good time keeping my eyes peeled for the swift-moving swallows who dart through the late afternoon collecting insects to feed their baby swallows. It's a truly amazing sight. The young birds—four in the mud nests their parents have made high on the walls of the Señor's studio—squawk loudly when they're hungry. They carry on so, you'd think they're near death. They open their mouths as wide as possible, the noise squeezing out of their throats while their mothers zoom about, grabbing up insect after insect, then carefully dropping them into the gaping mouths.

Mothers and fathers of all animals are truly amazing creatures. We cats are no exception. I think back to the time when I was a little baby kitten, helpless and meowing for something to eat. My mother would always take care of me. Today I watch mothers looking after their kittens and guarding them from harm in their boxes or baskets provided by their owners. In the garden they choose a soft grassy place carefully. The mothers always pick a place that's safe from predators or dogs who might do them harm.

The Señor has a book of cat photos. In it is a marvelous shot taken by a photographer in the middle of New York City. While traffic was at its peak, the lucky photographer caught a mother cat with her baby kitten in her mouth. Despite the hundreds of cars speeding by and the thousands of pedestrians, the mother is hell-bent on delivering her baby to safety. In the midst of this otherwise helter-skelter scene, traffic stops and people part to make a pathway for the pair. Proudly making her way, the small black-furred mother, her baby clutched in her mouth, proceeds to cross the impossible traffic-crowded street while people stare with incredulous expressions. It is a magnificent moment of triumph for an unlikely heroine making her indelible statement.

Where did she come from? Where was she going? Where were her other kittens? We will never know. And why did that courageous mother end up in a city as large as New York? Again, the answer is unknown. Such is the mystery of a good photograph. When unanswered questions appear in our minds, the photo becomes more than just a picture. To me, it becomes poetry. It makes that one moment memorable.

No matter where I go, I carry with me the image of that little cat and her baby, showing courage in the face of grave danger and not seeming to care. Although I have no memory of such a courageous event happening to me as a kitten, I am convinced that my mother— a proud Siamese—would have been capable of carrying off such a brave act.

The next time you see a mother cat moving her babies, watch how she carries them, one by one, gently lifting them by the neck, cradling them in her mouth, careful never to harm them. It is quite an art. Each time, it reminds me of how a Mexican mother rolls up her baby in her *rebozo* or shawl and ties it around her back and goes to work washing clothes or selling fruit on the street.

And each time I see a cat mother carrying her kittens or a Mexican *madre* with her *muchacha*, I think of that noble cat in New York.

BIRDS

Sing a song of sixpence, a pocket full of rye,
Four and twenty blackbirds baked in a pie.
When the pie was opened the birds began to sing.
Wasn't that a dainty dish to put before a king?

When the Señor was saying the old rhyme to a little boy one day, it made me think about birds. I don't know what rye is, but it's not the stuff in a bottle of liquor. It's some kind of grass, I think. And how did twenty-four blackbirds get into a pie?

Now that I'm a birdwatcher, I've been thinking a lot about birds these days. As a reformed birdnapper, I have taken it upon myself to study birds. We have many kinds in our garden and I try to remember them. One I really like to watch is the redheaded woodpecker. They call him a *carpintero*, which is carpenter in Spanish, because he chops a round hole in the trunk of a tree and makes a nest for himself and his family inside. We have many grackles. They're black birds with long tails. They squawk wildly and fight with each other, turning summersaults as they careen around the garden. Then there are beautiful sleek-backed doves, and nervous little hummingbirds that buzz in the air like overgrown bees, and small swallows. Every year they arrive for the winter, make their mud-daubed nests on the walls of the Señor's studio, lay their eggs, have their babies, and then they fly north at the end of winter. Next year they arrive again to repeat the process. I read in one of the Señor's books that many of these birds—particularly the hummingbirds—fly thousands of miles north for the spring and summer, then they find their way back, all the way to San Miguel, to our street and to our house. Some of the swallows have used the same nests for five years, arriving in the fall to patch up their former home with leaves, soft mud, and feathers. I believe that they have some sort of built-in radar

or computer in their little heads to direct them. It's not unlike the millions of butterflies who return to their forest home in Mexico every year.

This morning I awoke to hear different sounds of many kinds of birds. They make a joyful sound in the mornings. The rooster in the backside of the garden sings out his cockadoodledoo: "*Buenos dias!*" Good day. In her quiet coo, the dove replies: "*Buenos dias!*" The little swallow chirps in little staccato song. They all blend together in a morning melody, a sweet friendly welcome, starting the day with deep notes and warbling whistles, making me stand tall, stretch my legs and bow my back, fluffing my fur. Standing atop the high wall, the catbird pretends he's me, saying: "Meow, meow," and it gives me a chuckle, which is not a bad way to begin a good day.

A Zoo

If the Señor is not careful, soon he'll be running a zoo in his garden. The squirrels, the possums who wander freely through the underbrush, and the roosters and chickens, we're a regular menagerie. In the backside of the garden, the speckled rooster is the king. He came over our wall one day, decided he liked it here, and stayed. He even brought a hen wife from a nearby neighbor's yard. Alfredo found their nest under the thick bushes. In it were eggs. Alfredo, who loves birds and fowl, did not disturb the nest but watched it closely. Soon, five little chicks pecked out of their eggshells, and when sunlight struck their faces they began chirping loudly. Their tiny eyes opened and their mother brought worms and insects to feed them.

The chicks were just a few days old when another rooster, this one with shining black feathers, climbed over the wall and came looking for his wife. His cockledoodledoo was fierce. A shiver of fright came over the entire garden. He stepped high, his regal head with its bright red comb shifting about as his eyes darted first to focus on one corner, then on the other. Whiskers and Scruffy and I sat on the patio and watched, saying nothing, wondering if the Señor would hear the commotion. The first rooster, whose breast feathers were speckled and smooth as silk, came out of the brush with his own fine, pompous step. He strode directly to the invader, snapping his heels against the hard ground. He too held his head high and let out a fierce cry.

Both were cocks bred to fight. Mexicans raise them to fight in rings just as some raise thoroughbred horses to run fast. They usually do not bother other chickens, but when they come face-to-face, their instincts rise to the surface and they go at it spur-to-spur, snarling and snapping like well-trained prizefighters.

Within a moment, they were striking at each other with their leather-hard feet. The speckled rooster raised his beak and snapped at the black. The black jumped two feet off the ground and hit breast-high. The speckled fell back, teetered on his heels, then struck a blow with his feet.

Both toppled over, wrestled across the yard, let out several high-pitched cackles, then the black disappeared back over the wall as quickly as he had entered our universe.

As we were wondering what had happened so suddenly, we saw Alfredo walk onto the patio from his workshop. The strange rooster obviously did not want Alfredo to catch him in our garden.

Now the two roosters live in relative peace. Our speckled rooster lives with his hen wife and chicks in the garden behind the house. The black rooster lives on the other side of the wall with his family. In the morning, each begins with a loud cockledoodledoo. One sounds a loud alarm, then the other follows with an even louder sound. Sometimes they crow together. I use them as an alarm clock, starting the day at the crack of dawn.

Once I saw Florence chasing the chicks. At first, I was afraid for the little ones. Then I realized that Florence was just having fun. She frightened them when she first began her tricks, but they soon learned she was only being a playful cat. When Scruffy took up the same joshing, the rooster took after him, fluttering and pecking and cockledoodling in a fury.

Alfredo had thought about making a coop where he could keep the chicks, but they grew too fast. Before he could gather the materials, the chicks had grown into pullets. Before he knew it, they were laying eggs. Then he discovered the eggs were being stolen. They would lay their eggs in the bushes, then somebody, or some animal, would steal them. Also, the loose birds would eat our cat food before we could get to it. Alfredo, having more hens than he knew what to do with, began giving some to neighbors. He hates to do it. He loves his animals and birds. He finally made the cages, painted them bright blue and red, and had more inhabitants than he had space. Even after he gave some away, Alfredo spent a lot of time cleaning cages and keeping food and water for them. And when he approaches the cages, the hens cackle like crazy, knowing that soon they would have a clean place to walk, a pan filled with water and another filled with food.

There was once a bird artist who listed more than two hundred American birds in the book he illustrated. Imagine if we had two hundred kinds of cats. I know the encyclopedia lists ten or twelve cats, and we don't see all of the varieties very often. We do breed different colors and mixes, but we are not so different from each other like the birds. Not like the little tiny hummingbird and the big stork. Of course, being a Siamese is very special, as I have been telling you from the beginning of my tale. Some day you may be lucky enough to have a Siamese come and live with you. If you adopt a Siamese as a kitten, you will have the pleasure of getting to know each other while he's growing up. Or, you might adopt a full-grown Siamese, like I was taken in by the Señor, and you will discover that he will be very appreciative of your love and kindness to him. Or, you might find a stray cat that needs a home and he might turn out like Scruffy, who is now loving and affectionate toward the Señor, and maybe he appreciates his home maybe even more than Florence and me.

RHYTHMS & RHYMES

There are all sorts of rhythms and rhymes about cats. We've been the subject of numerous poems, songs, and chit-chats from the beginning of time.

"You've lost your mittens, you naughty kittens, and you shall have no pie," says the children's rhyme. What are mittens? Only for kittens? I didn't know, so I asked the computer, and it said "a form of glove made of wool to put on the hands in wintertime to keep warm." I've never seen mittens, because it's warm in Mexico and we don't need them.

Also on the computer, I discovered there are fancy pet boutiques that sell mittens for cats. In fact, my most recent email communications with Fluffy of Fifth Avenue informs me there are many such fashions about which I am ignorant. Fluffy says that when she leaves her owner's apartment, crosses the avenue and ventures into Central Park, she is faced with a winter wonderland of snow and ice. Just reading her communiqué, I shiver and feel cold all through my middle. Fluffy says when it becomes too windy, her owner fastens a fur coat around her body to protect her from the chill, and she cannot go out at all during December, January, or February without being covered in a sweater, wearing her knitted hat, and her mittens. At first, I thought it was because she is some kind of high-society female feline, but when she described the cold and wet, I knew it had to be more than that.

"Pusscat, pusscat, where have you been? I've been to London to see the

Queen," goes another rhyme. Sometimes Fluffy sends me new rhymes over the Internet. She's a very smart cat and sometimes I lay on the patio in the sunshine and dream about what she must look like. I think of her as a well-groomed Persian. In the summertime, I think of her in one of those fancy lacy gowns, highlighting the fluff of her very fine fur. I told her that I liked that line about London and the Queen. I've never been to London, but I think I should go some day. I could visit the Queen in one of her royal castles. I would get dressed up in a fine black silk tuxedo and have a black bowtie and white gloves or mittens. Perhaps I would wear a top hat. That would be something, don't you think? I'd tiptoe through the front portico like Fred Astaire in one of those old black-and-white musical movies that the Señor loves to watch on television. I would kneel in front of the Queen and she would tap my shoulder with her  bejeweled sword. It would be a grand ceremony in which the Queen would proclaim me "Sir Nobby" for one and all of her subjects to hear.

It's a splendid idea, I told Fluffy, and she agreed. But I told her not to bother about having her fine fur coiffured for the occasion. After all, I'm not going to London. If push comes to shove, I'll have Scruffy, Whiskers, and Florence as my audience when the Señor himself will proclaim me Sir Nobby for our little group.

Video Cat

The other day I saw myself on video. There I was, strutting my stuff, Sir Nobby himself, like the most sophisticated, handsome cat in the world. I'm telling you, I looked better than any cat actor who ever brightened the silver screen. I should be in Hollywood, California, the way I looked. I even *meow*-talked on the videotape and sounded like a feline Barrymore, my voice deep and manly and cultured. The video showed Ossito too, and he too came off as a very good actor, very natural, barking in a fine voice. We could perform as a pair, the Amazing Cat and Dog Show. Wasn't there a dog once named Rin Tin Tin? And a Felix the Cat? They were performers in the movies, before television came along. I certainly wouldn't mind doing a few commercials, if they paid me enough. I would parade before the camera and pronounce, "Sir Nobby prefers Cat-O, the new cat food with four vitamins and extra protein for very special animals like yours." I'd even nibble a few bites for the camera, smiling and showing my superior teeth. I would let the voice-over state how Cat-O had improved the sheen of my coat, although I cannot see where I need improving, since I am a splendid specimen of cat just the way I am.

The video showed Whiskers too, but she's camera shy and doesn't film very well. I wish Florence had been there. She is a true beauty. Although I'm not the demonstrative or lover type that Hollywood seems to prefer, I wouldn't mind doing a love scene with Florence. We could purr together, rub our cheeks close, and maybe even roll our eyes. I thought Scruffy might show up nicely as a juvenile delinquent who had gone wrong but who had learned to love the good life. I pictured him as a James

Dean cat, a rebel cat without a cause.

I take pride in what I do. I'm no scaredy-cat. I'm a top cat. I'm a star. Oh, I won't let my stardom go to my head. I'll let you decide how popular I am. You can email me and let me know exactly what you think of my looks on video— then we'll decide whether to put more cameras around the house. But I probably can't invite you here to interview me; there are already too many writers and photographers coming to interview the Señor about his work. He is very famous, you know, and photographers come with their new digital cameras that make it easy to take good shots. If you do come to see me, bring a good contract. And don't forget: Sir Nobby is copyrighted, so you must get permission to use me in your movies or advertising. There's only one Sir Nobby—and I'm he!

COMPUTER CAT

I was on the Internet! The Señor received a copy from a friend. When he clicked onto the name *Leonard Brooks*, an advertisement popped up onto the screen. A gallery was selling a painting the Señor did of me sitting next to a vase of flowers. The painting is called *Cat With Flowers*. I wasn't Sir Nobby back then, or surely he would have given it that title. Nevertheless, there I was for everybody to see, and a very handsome likeness to boot. Of course, if I had my druthers, I'd ask the Internet people to announce beneath the painting that the cat in the painting is actually a younger version of the now-famous new-age computer cat, Sir Nobby. If you have a reproduction of this work on your walls, I ask you to add this line, for clarification. If you are famous, why not let the world know, I say—like the movie stars do. It's good publicity. It's what will happen after my book is published and I get on the television programs. I wish Larry King could speak *meow*-talk but he can't, so I'll just have to study my English talk and learn a few more words to say instead of *yes* or *no* or *good day*. I'll listen to Oprah. She has good sounds, and I'm sure she will want me for an interview. It would be *purr*haps a first for her: a royal cat who has written a book. That would beat a hundred-year-old whose first novel is a Civil War epic or a fifteen-year-old whose memoir tells of her naughty exploits on the Riviera.

In the meantime, don't forget that you can contact me at Cat-SpeakMeowMeow.com, and I'll listen to your words.

EVOLUTION

id you ever study the story of evolution? I have. A most interesting topic. I found it in a double-page spread in the encyclopedia. The Señor had left the big book open and I just happened to wander upon it.

I looked down at a chart showing how man became man and woman became woman after millions of years of change. Pictures showed the first signs of life on the barren rocky earth. It was a surface like the moon. Nothing was alive. Then one day a tiny spot came to life. It grew larger and larger, all the while changing its form. First it was a tiny worm, then it became a caterpillar with wiggly legs. Some of the spots started to grow tiny wings. Millions of years later these tiny forms had branched out into many different forms.

As the chart continued, I saw how the artist showed the meaning of evolution: to evolve and change. When the great waters flooded the barren earth, some of the forms developed fins and became the first fish. To survive, they continued to change. Just as the earliest forms of life learned to live and breathe and move on the desolate earth, they grew and multiplied, and the first plants sprouted and soon trees began to grow, forming the first forest.

After millions more years, animals became enormous. Immense creatures, known as dinosaurs, roamed the earth and ate the forests. Because they were predators, they fought huge battles among themselves, killing each other. Then the first forms began coming out of the desert-like environment, but the dinosaurs did not change and, generation after generation, they soon disappeared. Now our scientists find their huge bones and skeletons buried in the earth, and you can actually see them reassembled in museums in countries all over the globe. We have many movies that show how they stalked the earth. Did you see *Jurassic Park*? It showed how one scientist reinvented the dinosaur and his huge animal relatives and put them in a park for tourists to enjoy. It was very eerie and frightening.

Even after the dinosaur became extinct, some of their relatives changed into what became the elephant and hippopotamus. With them, other animals began to emerge on our planet. Some came out of the great flood that engulfed most of the earth's surface. When the water began to subside, fish that had formed in the water crawled out of the sea and grew legs and eventually some grew wings and began to fly short distances. Birds evolved out of these meager beginnings. Then lizards formed four legs and snakes began to crawl about the plants that developed in the sunlight. Those with legs learned to climb into the newly formed trees and found insects for food.

At about this time, monkey-like animals were formed and climbed into trees with the lizards. They learned to eat fruit and vegetation. From time to time, many animals, insects, fish, birds, and all types began to live from the land and from each other.

Somewhere in the process, the cat appeared. The lemur was the most intelligent of all. While monkeys learned to chatter monkey-talk, swinging from tree to tree with their

families, the lemur is shown on the Señor's charts as the most intelligent.

One day a miracle happened. A monkey decided he was tired of walking stooped over on all four paws. It seemed ridiculous to him that he should scamper about in such a state. He stood erect, tested his balance on his two hind legs. At first, he wavered to and fro. Other monkeys watched in amazement. Then he took a step, teetered again, but did not fall. Next he took three quick steps. The other monkeys chattered in exasperation, watching his stunt. Then he walked a dozen steps, turned and looked back and grinned widely, laughing and chiding the others for their cowardice. Within a short while, the monkey, who began to look more and more like man as we know him, began to strut upon the stage of the jungle. Soon, others tried to copy his actions. Some became big fierce monkeys called gorillas and became a dominant force in the jungle.

The first human beings didn't talk and live like we do today. That took thousands upon thousands of years.

The lemur and lions and tigers still walk and stalk other animals, killing and eating them in order to survive. From these wild creatures, a more sedate and lovable feline broke away from the others and became cats like we are today. We do not stand up on our hind legs—except on occasion, when we want to be cute for our human owners. We didn't change the way we live, although we depend on our human masters for food and water. Like dogs, who evolved from wolves into the domesticated, friendly pets who learned to live with humans, we too became friendly felines who love our owners.

Are we still evolving? I believe that human brains keep changing. Humans continue to find new ways to live. They invent things to make their lives easier, like air-conditioning to fight hot weather, and stoves to combat the cold. They design fancy new houses and gardens. Right here in San Miguel, architects build modern houses of steel and glass that hang onto the sides of the hills high above town. And artists like the Señor are always looking at the world with different and more unusual visions, and their designs decorate both the new homes and the ancient ones that are being renovated in the four-hundred-year-old *centro* of our town.

Although many people around the world have learned to live together, many others have never learned to accept peace as a way of life. People still kill each other. They cannot seem to elevate themselves to a level where peace is the norm.

Although man has invented ways to transport himself from place to place in a fast and comfortable manner, he finds it necessary to fight to obtain oil to run the engines in jet airplanes, trains, trucks, buses, and automobiles. It's enough to make a thoughtful cat to wonder.

When I see on the television and the Internet where millions of humans around the world are starving and living in poverty, it makes me wonder whether all of man's inventions and all of his new discoveries have truly changed the world into a better and kinder place. Although many new religions have formed and sects and cults speak different tongues of peace and prosperity, the world still has not improved for those who are hungry.

While I am at it, I would like to interject my worry about drugs in our society. Cats don't smoke marijuana or sniff glue or snort anything but a good supply of catnip, which is enough to make us really feel good. It is not harmful, does not elevate our blood pressure or quicken our pulse. However, now and then I see a frisky young cat stepping about sniffing certain plants, and it is becoming a distasteful bad habit. Cats don't drink alcohol like humans, but catnip can make us drunk, if we abuse it, and kittens don't realize this. I've told our cat clan that they should instruct the young as early as possible. Otherwise, they might abuse catnip without realizing what is happening. *Purr*haps if the gardener will dig up the catnip plants in our garden it will help. But I've noticed how the young look for the stuff in all of the gardens, not just ours.

I know that I am lucky to be a cat. As you can see by my wonderings, some day I will be a preacher cat. Not a Sir. The Reverend Nobby will go out among the multitudes. He will tell all cats how to become better cats. He will point out many human foibles. He will say that it is possible—in a *purr*fect world—for cats to dominate. We will stop all terrorism and violence, all fighting in foreign countries, and it will be a marvelous, peaceful, joyful world for everyone.

I have a dream, where cats of all *purr*suasions will walk hand-in-hand among humans—and I know as a computer cat that such a dream is not impossible—although it might take centuries to become a reality.

Nobby's Note: Now I will share my memoirs with my friend Whiskers, who wishes to put in a word or two.

WHISKERS TALKS

I'm not a Siamese cat, like my friend Sir Nobby. He's an aristocat, you know. But I am a nice black-and-white, good-looking lady cat. I have grown up since I first entered the Señor's house. Like our friend Scruffy, I came from a very poor background. Unlike Scruffy, however, I knew my parents. My mother, who always had a hard time making do, taught me early on to take care of myself, to stay clean and steer clear of ruffians. My father, Tabby, was a roustabout cat, if you know what I mean; he went out at night, roaming the streets and the underbrush of Juarez Park.

I watched the Señor's house from a distance. Even as a kitten I knew I would love to live in his nice house. One day when the door was left open, I slipped inside. I hid, waiting in the shadows, and when Nobby wasn't around I stole some of his food and lapped up his water.

During my third day in the house, Nobby caught me at his bowl. He meowed a stern warning and brought my presence to the attention of the Señor, who reached down and picked me up and stroked my fur. "You're a pretty little thing," he said, and I purred as pretty as you please.

At first Nobby ignored me. He walked away, acting as though he didn't even know I was there. I discovered, watching him, that he is a grand actor. I believe he would make a very good movie star, if the right part came his way. Sometimes, I think he knows it too.

During those first few days, whenever the Señor reached down and picked me up and placed me in his lap, Nobby strutted across some of the Señor's unfinished paintings. "Nobby," he exclaimed. "You know better than that!"

After a short while, I came to realize that Nobby was only vying for attention. He loves the Señor and doesn't want him to share his affections with others. During those times, Nobby went out of his way to please the Señor. He even rubbed next to the Señor's calves, purring and pushing his head against the Señor's leg. I knew it was his way of telling the master that he was *numero uno* in this house. And he let me know it too.

When he saw that the Señor was pleased with my presence, Nobby slowly made friends with me, wanted to know where I came from and who my parents were. I did not inquire about his lineage, but he let me know that he was born of nobility that went back for many generations.

Soon Nobby let me jump up on the bed and scratch his favorite scratchy places on a favorite chair or sofa. Sometimes he even let me play football with him, kicking the ball my way and letting me fetch it for him. But generally Nobby is very standoffish. He even gets angry and chases me around the room, throwing me onto my side and growling, showing his teeth. Sometimes I'll jump on him when he is taking his catnap. And when I awaken him suddenly, he gets angry. But he never stays angry.

During the year I've been here I've grown larger. It's not as easy for Nobby to toss me onto my side, although he is still bigger than I. My whiskers and eyebrows have grown very long. That's why I'm called Whiskers.

I have learned a lot since I came to live in this fine house. I've made friends with Scruffy. I don't chase Alfredo's new little chicks. I try to behave myself with the birds in the garden. I am always affectionate with the Señor. I meowed sympathetically when he had to go to the doctor to have a cyst removed from his face. When he came home that afternoon I rubbed next to him and purred and lay near his side. Sometimes, when I think he's sad, I do a trick, tumbling over sideways, to cheer him up. I'll bite his shoes and roll my eyes when he looks down at me, and I'll rub next to his leg and let him pet me and caress my velvet ears.

Nobby doesn't show him affection like I do, although I know he feels sorry for the Señor at times. Nobby is very reserved. He's a male aristocat, while I'm a lady cat. We of the female feline species are just naturally more loving.

FLORENCE

From the beginning, I wondered about Florence. She is a pretty little common cat. Like Whiskers, she is what humans refer to as "a mixed breed." When Florence is up to no-good, she runs off with Tabby, who considers himself her husband. Once she ran off for several days and came back and took over the back stoop just like she'd always done. She lords over Whiskers. She always assumes the older sister role, like their mother had been better to her than to Whiskers, although Whiskers has assured me that was not the case at all.

It's times like these when I become a social arbiter. I wanted to tell the Señor he shouldn't be so forgiving of Florence, but I let well enough alone. I thought it would be better if Florence and Whiskers took care of their own problem without my interference.

Then the Señor leaned back in his favorite thick-cushioned chair and I crawled into his lap. He told us about visiting a great American photographer on his *rancho* in California. The great and famous man was in the last days of his life, sitting in a wheelchair surrounded by dozens of cats. With him was a young woman who cared for him and all the cats. All of these cats, strays and purebreds, were allowed to sleep inside or go wherever they wanted. "There were so many cats," the Señor said. "They had literally taken over the place. The feeding for all of them had to be enormous." The man's sons tried to remedy the problem, but the old man would have none of their interference and the cats were allowed to stay. The young woman had photographed the old man and all of the cats, and these photos were included in a book. And even though they had become famous after the book's publication, the Señor said he could not stay in the stuffy house more than a few minutes because of the horrendous odor. Hearing him describe the situation, I wrinkled my nose and shook my head. And the Señor agreed that I would not have enjoyed such living conditions.

The Señor said he had enough cats. What with me and Whiskers, Florence and Tabby, and Scruffy now and then, we were a house-full.

I knew that if all of the cats were Siamese it would be a different story. Siamese are decent housebroken animals, not the type to spray every corner or leave droppings on the floor. We are domesticated creatures who do not overstay our welcome and never sleep on the bed unless we're invited.

I began thinking about the pioneer cats of the past. There were many brave and faithful individuals who took off with adventurous families in their wagons across the vast prairie, fording streams and following little-known pathways through the mountains. These cats traveled from the eastern seaboard of North America to the wilds of the west. They slept outside, like their families, searched for water, withstood freezing cold and icy snow, and, because they endured such severe hardship, ended up on a settler's property. Just as dogs accompanied many pioneer families, so did cats. Sometimes they had to run and hide from fierce Indians or wild animals. Occasionally, when cats were frantic to escape mutilation or death, they became lost in the unmapped country. Of course, this was long before cars and gasoline stations, where travelers today can stop and ask directions. Back then, one of my ancestors joined in such a trek but he kept no journal. Cats were not blessed with computers like the one on which I am writing my tale. So his memories were never recorded. However, when I was very young and he was very old, he told me about traveling to California. There, he raised a family and many of his progeny have become movie stars, although dogs in that "New West" world got first billing. Lassie and Rin Tin Tin and a little mutt named Toto were given star roles and top publicity, but the old Siamese told me about numerous beautiful well-bred cats who had walk-on roles in some of Hollywood's finest early films. Because dogs barked loudly, wagged their tails, and moaned demonstratively deep in their throats, the moviemakers gave them the best roles. But that was long before my old uncle made his way down to Baja and then across the mainland to the east coast of Mexico, where I was born.

I'd say my cat-friends and I have a *purr*fect life. I have my routine. I go out in the morning for a stroll in the garden, find the pile of sand Alfredo keeps for us, tromp across the pathway we've made through the thickest underbrush where sometimes I imagine I am in a jungle in deepest dark Africa—then, as I settle under the window of Alfredo's studio where he's carving a musician playing a violin, I take an easy cat-nap to the rhythm of his work. I don't know why people often say, "It's a dog's life," when they refer to paradise.

After my nap, I came across Scruffy climbing out of the hole where he sleeps because it reminds him of his old home on the bank of the filthy *arroyo*. I chased him across the garden, where we spotted a squirrel that we both chased up a tree. We got five or six feet up the trunk before I gave up and inched my way back down.

Scruffy, however, didn't stop until he was nestled in a wedge between two limbs. He yawled loudly, struck out with his paw, but the squirrel just laughed and jumped to the branch of another tree to make his escape.

In the meantime, Scruffy looked around and down. He reached out but could not find a way to climb down to safety. I watched and meowed directions, but I could see by his expression that he was bumfuzzled. Poor Scruffy didn't know what to do. He was captured in the tree the way I had been held hostage in the cage. But I couldn't help him. I knew if I climbed up and tried to free him I would probably end up in the same predicament. Then there would be two of us up the tree instead of just one.

I told Scruffy to relax and try to figure out what to do next, but he only growled at me and said it was easy for me to say—I was not the cat up a tree.

"Hold steady," I told him, and scampered off to find Alfredo.

After some frantic *meow*-talk and the shaking of my head to make him know I was serious, Alfredo dropped his carving and followed me to the tree on the far side of our garden, where he immediately saw the problem.

Alfredo tried to reach up to the limb where Scruffy was stuck, but it was too high. Scruffy tried to squirm himself loose, but he only slid down and made the situation worse, the two branches squeezing beneath his front two legs, making it impossible for him move.

"Hold on, *mi amigo*," Alfredo said. "I'll be right back."

From the tool shed, he quickly retrieved a ladder, which he then steadied against the trunk of the tree. As he climbed, he spoke softly to Scruffy. Finally, he was able to reach out and cup Scruffy's lower body in his big hands. Alfredo has an artist's hands—long fingers and big palms. His hands are very strong, but very gentle. He lifted Scruffy up, up, and up, until the limbs released his legs.

Alfredo held him securely next to his own body as he climbed down.

"*Como esta?*" Alfredo asked, placing Scruffy on the grass next to me.

Scruffy *meow*-answered his thank you, shivered anxiously, and took an uneasy step. After stumbling, he steadied himself, shook his body again, and tested his running legs. After a few steps, he was his old self. He turned and looked at me and winked. I knew he would soon be up to his old tricks.

I rubbed against Alfredo's legs to let him know how much we appreciated his help. Then, I went over to where Florence lay sleeping, unaware of the drama that had just unfolded in our midst. After watching Scruffy romp for a few moments, I curled up next to Florence. Before closing my eyes, I thought how wonderful it is just to be alive. Listening to Florence purr, I felt happy with our blessed world here in our garden in San Miguel.

After a short nap, I awakened to hear the Señor having his breakfast. I went inside, had a taste of my fresh food that he'd put out, did some self-grooming, then went into the room where he was eating. I rubbed next to his legs and he leaned down and stroked my side. "You're a good old boy, Nobby," he said, and I *meow*-answered that he was about the best Señor a Mexican cat could have.

Poor Florence

P oor Florence! She's been alone since Tabby ran off one night and didn't come home. If you ask me, he went off tomcatting and got lost down in some barrio where the catnappers had taken me. But there is no one out there in the world to pay a reward for Tabby. And he doesn't have a good friend to brave danger and save him the way Scruffy came to my rescue.

I never talked much with Tabby. He was one of those somber, silent types, when he wasn't running wild through an alleyway or *arroyo*. He was pleasant enough, but he kept to himself and didn't interfere in other people's lives. He came over the wall on his own one day when he was looking for a new place to live. He had been sleeping on the porch of an empty house and was very lonely and extraordinarily hungry. He didn't like being called a "stray" but it was not all his fault. The person who'd been taking care of him moved away and left him all by himself.

When he met Florence, who was another stray and also very lonely, they decided to live in the Señor's garden, if they weren't chased away.

Back then, Ossito the dog was still alive. Unlike the way he acted toward most intruders, he didn't chase Florence and Tabby. He watched them closely and made the decision that, as far as he was concerned, they were okay. It was his way of welcoming them to our world.

When the Señor saw them, he asked in *meow*-talk, "Who are you two? You both look very hungry." He went inside and got a heaping plate of cat food and brought it outside and put it down next to my bowl.

At first they were too shy to eat, but I noticed how Tabby glared at the food. I knew he was terribly hungry. The Señor, sizing up the situation, stepped back inside and left us all alone. Ossito lay on his old blanket and watched. I moved over close to Ossito to let Florence and Tabby know we would not stop them.

With no obvious interference, Tabby was the first to go to the plate and begin eating. In a few moments, Florence joined him.

After Tabby ran away, Florence missed him terribly. She sighed deeply and lay down and closed her eyes. After she awakened the second time, she didn't move from her resting place. Her eyes surveyed the garden. Later, she told me, "He will return soon. I know he will. Tabby loves me."

Every morning she fixes her eyes on the top of the wall. I know she is expecting him to appear. But so far he has stayed away.

Whiskers and I try to cheer her up, but she doesn't pay much attention to our antics. She is very sad, but we keep hoping her sadness will vanish soon.

PAINTING

Today I tried to paint a picture. I've watched the Señor many times with his sketchpad. His hands work quickly, moving faster than a squirrel skittering away from Scruffy. He begins with simple lines, curlicues of shapes and forms, then he begins to shade areas, and before you know it, like magic, the scene that you see beyond is recreated on paper.

Oftentimes he will come into the garden and set up his easel, like he did on the seashore when I was a small cat near Tampico. He takes his paint tray and begins to dip his brush into one color, then another, sometimes mixing and matching.

For me, it started by accident. My tail swished over a palette of acrylic paints on the Señor's studio table, where I had jumped up to see what was there. There was a piece of watercolor paper on the table, so I decided I would try it out. I would brush on some color the same way the Señor does. I tried it out, then looked at my design. An idea took form, and I tried again with a new color.

It was fun! I don't know how to draw. Oh, I've heard the Señor talking about all of the things he does, explaining to his artist friends about various art styles. The Señor is very knowledgeable about all aspects of art. He has used many techniques and art professors from Canada and the United States have come to San Miguel to listen to his words and watch his techniques. Some students sit in the large *sala* and take notes while the Señor tells them about all of the things he has learned during his many years as an artist.

While I can't draw a straight line, I can certainly twist my tail in a curve, and I think the results look good on the canvas. I do the same thing many other artists do: splash paint onto canvas. It's called abstract painting. Mine is just as good as many others who have drawn national and international acclaim.

What I am doing is called self-expression. I wiggle my tail through the paints. Then I swish it over the canvas, making my oblong and obtuse shapes, using different colors—sometimes more than a half-dozen. One move connects with another until the entire canvas is filled with color.

On another day in the studio, I walked across the canvas. When I I pushed my paw into another color, where I had stepped. When I looked expressive stroke of my very unique

dipped my paw into the paint and looked back, there were paw-prints. then I raked it across the places at the image, I knew that was a good paintbrush.

I can't manage the delicate watercolors. Sometimes he just brush. Then he stands back and strokes that the Señor puts into his barely touches the paper with his studies it. Then he might touch it again. Or, he might nod and put his brush down. *Purr*haps watercolor is too difficult for me now. However, I might try it in the future.

For now, my strokes are bold and generous. When paint is left out on the palette, I go for it. It's my time to be expressive. My big furry paw makes a strong, forceful impression.

*Purr*haps one day I will even have a one-cat show like the paintings elephants and the monkeys have had in shows in New York galleries. When the critic for the *New York Times* writes about my show, he might call my abstracts "abscats," and sing my praises as the newest trend in the art world. *Purr*haps even art historians will write dissertations about the depth of my work. And some day a group of Scandinavians might pick my overall work for a great award and the Señor will be very proud of me and our photo will be in all of the

newspapers and CNN and FOX News will do programs on my work.

The same critics who praise the blank canvases hanging in some museums will laud me as magnificent and great and worthwhile. *Purr*haps I will simply allow the Señor to hang one of my blank canvases. It will be one on which I will step without bothering to dip my paw into the paint. It will be "The Vast Universe of Nothingness," an illustrious masterpiece by Sir Nobby, the greatest cat-artist of all time.

Such would be "a happening" and I will be known far and wide as the most fashionable cat in the art world. We will make the entire community of artists, art historians, art scholars, and other interested parties realize that there is no necessity whatsoever in the old-fashioned stuff called paint. Paint would become passé.

They would all point toward me and know that I am not just up-to-date, as they say about some artists, but leading the pack. One art journalist might write: "Sir Nobby is the Lone Ranger of the art world. He is out there on the far horizon, showing all of the others how it is done when you have true imagination and fortitude."

I can see the headlines now: "Cat Scores Hit. Remarkable Show of Cat-onic Collage. Canvases Untouched or Spoiled. A Pure Statement Well Worth Seeing."

I can see the people in line to enter the gallery. Each has been sold a catalog for $10. The public scans the blank pages. They *ooh* and *aah* and whisper enthusiastic remarks. They are eager to squeeze through the door and have a look for themselves. They would be my adoring, appreciative public. The only sign of a scratch in the catalog is Sir Nobby's signature on the cover: a cat's paw. Some enthusiasts purchase two and three catalogs as souvenirs or collector's items.

NOTHING

by Sir Nobby

CATTY REMARKS

I try to never make catty remarks about my friends. Sometimes those around me cannot help themselves. When I knocked over a bowl of roses on the table and broke one of the Señor's favorite pink-shaded vases, he shook his head and said he considered it a "catastrophe." I shivered slightly and moved off into a corner, where I hoped to be invisible.

After he cooled down, I cat-tipped over to him and rubbed near his side to let him know I was sorry for my careless actions. He looked askance, then worked a smile onto his face. "Oh, Nobby," he finally said. Then he ran his fingers along my fur and let me cuddle close to his side. He is a very forgiving owner.

Sometimes it seems as though Whiskers, Florence, Scruffy, Tabby, and I are into everything. Our collective philosophy has always been "curiosity never killed the cat" and *purr*haps it is that reason why we seem to always get into trouble these days.

Whiskers was doing some minor-league exploring in the studio the other day when his shoulder hit a framed picture that was leaning against the wall. Before Whiskers could move to straighten it, the picture tumbled and the glass shattered. Luckily, Whiskers jumped back fast

enough and wasn't injured. But the Señor, who was working at the far end, looked up and shouted, "Whiskers! What are you doing?" We all knew he didn't want an answer. He already knew what Whiskers had been doing. That picture was the great one of Nobby the First which had been reproduced and sold all over the United States, Canada, and much of Europe. As I tiptoed by, moving out of the way, I could almost see the catastrophic grin on the face of Nobby the First in the painting.

SNOWCAT

Winter in San Miguel. Only a few days before Christmas. When I went out into the garden this morning for my early constitutional, I couldn't believe my eyes. Everything was white! The trees and plants had icy coatings and the hills beyond our walls were covered with a sheath of white snow. At first I thought I was imagining things. As you know by now, I have a *purr*fectly wonderful imagination. But this was real! When I put my paws onto the ground the cold shivered up through my legs. I wished I had mittens.

As soon as the damp cold hit, I picked up my gait. I stepped high, trotting about in the snow, kicking it up with my paws, watching the frosty flakes cloud up behind me. *Purr*ty soon, Whiskers and Scruffy joined me, dancing about in circles, kicking up more snow, our bodies invigorated with the cold and its visual effects.

I'd heard the Señor talk about the time the snow came ten or twelve years ago. That was before I came to San Miguel. It was back when Nobby the First reigned as emperor of this garden. Although Mexico is a tropical country, up here in the highlands we do have an occasional bout of cold in December and January. That year, the Señor said, journalists and photographers came to San Miguel, and the day the snow fell became headlines.

After we had our romp in the snow, we went inside to warm our paws and get some food the Señor had placed in the toasty kitchen for us.

Later in the morning, three young boys, sons of friends of the Señor, came

 over and played in the garden. Whiskers and Scruffy and I watched from the big windows as they played in the snow. One, who had lived in Canada and who was familiar with snow, showed the others what to do. He started a ball of snow rolling, collecting more snow and becoming bigger and bigger until it was the size of a human body. Then they rolled a smaller ball and stuck it on top of the larger one and it became a head. They stuck two pieces of stone in the smaller ball to make its eyes and tree branches on each side of the large ball to make arms. They fashioned a corncob pipe and stuck it in the snowman's mouth. When they did, Whiskers and Scruffy and I chuckled our delight and went outside to examine their sculpture closer. It was amazing and delightful to us, and we scampered around and around the snowman, dancing with its creators who were as delighted as we with their accomplishment.

I had heard the Señor and his Canadian artist friends talk about acquaintances of theirs in the northern country where ice-sculptors competed to see who could make the most elaborate design from ice. They did this out-of-doors in the freezing weather.

With this in mind, I tried my paw at such work. I rolled a small ball of snow with my cold paws and started my own sculpture. While Whiskers and Scruffy paw-pawed me and went back into the warm room, I remained outside to try and *purr*fect what I had started. Once my ball was finished, rolled until it was hard as a rock, I rolled another smaller ball, hardened it in the same manner, then I placed it just so on the tip edge of the larger ball. I shaped four legs and worked them beneath the larger ball. Within minutes, although my paws were nearly frozen, I placed two small stones in the small ball for eyes, fixed a curly piece of fern on the rear for a tail, and found two snippet ends of a fern that made *purr*fect ears. It was almost like working with clay to form a figure and similar to the way Alfredo carves some of his pieces. And, like the Señor's sketching, soon all of the pieces fit together and, like magic, I had made a real snowcat.

From the other side of the frosty window I saw Whiskers and Scruffy watching me. I couldn't help but think they were amused and amazed and maybe even slightly jealous. But they made no move to join me. The least they could do, I thought, was alert the Señor to bring his camera and take some pictures. But they didn't. They just sat there in the warmth and watched.

When I went inside they meowed their praise. I only nodded in an abbreviated way, letting them know I had not yet finished. From the kitchen closet I took several whisks from the broom. I took them outside and placed them just so on each side of my snowcat's nose.

This time when I entered the house my audience meowed their wholehearted approval.

On the following morning, when I went to see my work, all I found was stones and limbs and whisks lying on the ground. All of the snow had disappeared in the early sunlight. By mid-morning it was warm and time for a nap. Before I closed my eyes I hoped I wouldn't have to wait another ten or twelve years for another snowfall. It was a fun time.

In the aftermath of my snowy experience I did a lot of thinking about people who live in the Snow World. The Señor told about his time as a youngster in Canada, where snow fell in droves and stayed on the ground throughout the winter. He told about the far northland where the Inuit Eskimos make their homes from snow, like a huge snowball hollow on the inside. They call their homes "igloos" and

 they sleep, cook, and live in them. They dress in animal furs and hunt seals to use the blubber for food, and oil for fires to keep warm in their igloos. Some of the Inuit make sculptures from snow and ice, some very elaborate and greatly detailed.

A Cat's Christmas

I love Christmas. Here in Mexico we have Christmas *posadas*, nine nights with parades in which children from different streets and neighborhoods walk with bands of musicians and sing holiday songs. It's exciting to venture out into the streets that have been decorated with banners and *piñatas*. The parade stops while the children scramble to break the colorful *piñatas* with sticks. At Christmas, unlike birthdays, the children who strike at the *piñatas* are not blindfolded. As they strike,

a man on the roof of the house manipulates the *piñata* up and down, making it difficult to hit. But when a solid blow is struck, the goodies scatter through the air. Everyone reaches for candy, cookies, or some other prize. Sometimes the big boys rush in, grab the best prizes, and run away with them. Then the parade moves on to another neighborhood.

COMPUTER CAT WANDERS

As you have witnessed, from time to time my mind wanders. If I feel like singing, I sing. When I feel like dancing, I dance. I'm a poetic cat. I have my thoughts about this world and I don't keep them to myself. In fact, I am a very complicated cat. But I am also a committed cat. *What am I committed to?* Myself, that's who. Oh, I enjoy my world. It's a wonderful world. And mine is a wonderful life. I would give anything for my friends: the Señor, Whiskers, Scruffy, Florence, Alfredo, the roosters, and all the others.

We cats are strange animals. Rather crazy at times, as you know by now, but not half as crazy as humans. The longer I live with people the less I understand them and their ways. Especially people who call themselves "artists," as many of the Señor's friends call themselves. Every day I hear tales of how they live and think, and I cannot believe some of the things I hear or read. Art schools, for instance. They were once places where young people went to learn from experienced artists how to draw and use paint to make paintings. The same was true with schools for musicians and composers and for poets to learn to use words—and which words to use and not to use. Today, all has changed.

The Señor's niece wants to be an artist. She attended art school last year. Did she learn to draw and paint? Did they teach her anything about the history of art? All of her time was spent learning the art of NOT learning the basics. "Forget the basics!" the teachers taught. "Don't learn to draw!" Instead, they taught her about "happenings" and "installations." One student masterpiece that won a first prize was called "Room Divider." It consisted of a piece of string stretched across an empty room.

The professor judge wrote that it was "truly an original concept."

According to the Señor, the precedent for this judgment was the Turner Bequest at the Tate Gallery, where the jury gave first prize to an artist whose exhibit was an empty room in which the lights blinked on and off every few minutes. "Turner must be turning over in his grave," the Señor commented when he read about this situation.

And I agree completely. The *very* idea! As a cat who has lived among true artists, I have learned that millions of dollars are paid to people who can toss a ball into a basket, to others who shout and scream into microphones, men and women who say dirty words on television, and some who jump up and down and scream filthy epithets into microphones for the world of recorded music. I've never seen a feline rock star, but I'm sure there's one out there somewhere, waiting to be discovered.

CALLING A COMPUTER CONFERENCE

With all of this in mind, I decided I'd call for a cat computer conference. It is time for the intelligent cats in the universe to gather together. How can we do this? By computer, of course. Those of us who are smart enough to *meow*-talk can dance upon a laptop keyboard and move a mouse with our paw. So now is the time to spread the word for such a get-together.

In the beginning, I started with the cats of our known world. We all met in our garden on Thursday night a half-hour after sunset.

"Okay, here's the deal," I told the dozen who managed to get away from their homes to attend the meeting. "I will volunteer to be chair-cat-person, if you would like for me to take the bull by the horns."

"What bull?" asked Scruffy.

"Not a real bull," I told him. "It's only a figure of speech."

"Oh, I was hoping we'd have a cat bullfight and I could be the cat-matador."

"No!" I stated. "From now on, if you want to be recognized, raise your paw. I'll call your name and you may speak. Otherwise, you'll be out of order. Is that understood?"

They all nodded.

"We'll conduct our meeting according to *Cat's Rules of Order*. Only one cat can have his say at any one time."

I soon told them the purpose of our meeting: to *purr*suade a company to produce a cat computer. "If a company did, we'd give it a great deal of publicity. If it's successful, the company will make a lot of money. We would ask *purr*mission to go on the air and develop a website for ourselves where we can write free e-mails from one cat to another."

Several cats expressed opposition to the idea, saying it was way too far out for common cats in a small town like San Miguel de Allende, but Scruffy, Whiskers, and even Florence said they thought I was progressive in my approach, asking for universal understanding. I appreciated their support and told them so.

"After all," I told the group, "the guy who first came up with the idea of radio was told that it was a crazy idea. Now, almost every cat in the world can hear a radio for at least several hours every day. If we get an e-mail franchise, we could communicate with cats throughout the world with little or no effort. It is time for cats to have our say. If we can connect, we may even have a United Cat Front across the globe."

A PURRFECT DAY

I am happy today. A truly happy and contented cat. I woke up this morning purring and meowing to myself. It was so lovely I went outside to say a good meow to all of my cat friends. Everyone was smiling and said they were glad to see me. It seemed that they too had had a great night's sleep. In the fresh early morning air I smelled the jasmine flowers and orange blossoms. Florence welcomed me, and Whiskers joined in our tour of the garden. We could hear Scruffy caterwauling on the other side of the wall and knew he was having a good time giving chase to a squirrel or possum. The rooster was waiting and joined me in eating breakfast from the same bowl. Eight chicks followed him, looking so cute. This morning they were not the least bit afraid of me, and I kept my distance, simply admiring their plump little bodies. Somewhere beyond them two doves were cooing back and forth to each other. Across the lovely clear blue sky a giant white heron flapped his great wings and landed in one of our trees.

I settled on a bench, tucked my front paws under my chin, and thought about all the pleasant hours I had ahead of me on this *purr*fectly wonderful day. I would enjoy my good fortune of being a part of the Señor's household. I'm healthy and wealthy, I told myself. After all, I have all the love a mature cat could possibly want. Now I'm a wise old cat. I forgot about being Sir Nobby, the aristocat. I was simply a good, obedient, thankful cat. I would help all of my cat friends to be the best cats they could possibly be.

I played ball with Whiskers and she really enjoyed the romp.

Then I lay on the patio in the sunshine and gave myself a real genuine cat-washing that made me feel like a million dollars after our exercise.

After a mid-morning nap, I came inside and found the piano open, so I jumped up and tapped out a Gershwin tune. At least, that's what it was to me. It was a happy song that I felt all the way down to the tips of my paws.

Later, when I awakened on the sofa and found the Señor sketching me, I didn't move an inch so that he could finish. Then I let him stroke my ears and *meow*-talk about how handsome I looked.

I didn't look at the television that evening. I didn't want to be reminded of the horrible happenings in other parts of the world. As far as I was concerned, our world was *purr*fect, and I wanted to keep it that way.

I dozed again and dreamed of all the fun things I'd do tomorrow.

Sir Nobby R.A.

I hate surprises. Once, on my birthday, I came strolling into the garden and Scruffy, Whiskers, Florence, and several others jumped out of their hiding places, shouting, "Happy Birthday!" I thought I would fall over from fright. Of course, I smiled and told them, "Thank you," but my heart was racing ninety-to-nothing. I crawled through our door, thinking I would go inside and find a quiet place on the sofa where I could relax, but the Señor and several of his friends were there with a birthday cake for me. What can a cat do? I pranced about and rubbed against their legs and received their petting hands and ate the salmon pie they had gotten especially for me. And when the mariachis stopped by and played and sang "Las Mananitas" for me I tucked my chin down against my chest and tried to look like a cute cat.

But today I learned something that took me completely by surprise. The Señor called me into the house and began what I thought at first might be a stern lecture. I tried to think what I had done wrong, but absolutely nothing came to mind.

He was halfway into his spiel when I began listening to his words carefully. Unknown to me, the Señor had found one of my paintings on the floor of his studio several weeks ago. He had picked it up and carried it over to the light and examined it in great detail.

"When I saw the brushstrokes you had accomplished with such a fine paw, Nobby, I was amazed. It was by far your best work. It showed a superb eye, a strong hand, and a totally unique point-of-view. After I looked at it for several days, deciding you didn't need to do another thing to it—

sometimes an artist can overwork a painting—I decided I would take it with some of my own work to the Royal Academy. If I think it's that good, I told myself, why not let a jury of experts look it over and make a judgment?

"Well, they didn't question for a second the title, 'Sir Nobby: A Self-Portrait.' I watched as they hesitated in front of the canvas. They whispered among themselves as they put their faces down close and examined every last tiny detail. Then they backed away and tilted their heads and looked at it from every angle.

"Nobby, not only did they like your work, they have hung it on the walls of the National Gallery near some of my own best work."

I was beside myself. What a wonderful surprise! I was actually hanging on the walls of a great gallery where the Señor was recognized as one of the greatest painters of his time.

"And now, Sir Nobby," the Señor stated in his most exalted voice—a voice he did not often use with me or any other animal in our menagerie. "It is my distinct pleasure to inform you that you have been nominated to become a member of the Royal Academy."

I almost dropped my chin, but didn't. I held myself properly aloof, although I did cock my head to the side in what I thought was a regal pose.

As the Señor draped a royal blue velvet robe over my shoulders, it was all I could do to hold a tear within my eye. I told myself that I could not allow my feline friends to see me shed a tear on such an occasion. But it did indeed move me as he pinned the purple and gold ribbon and medal onto the breastwork of the robe.

Then he handed me a diploma making me an official associate member of the Royal Academy, where the Señor was a full-fledged member. He spoke about how happy he was that I was now a member, although as a cat I would not be able to attend the annual meetings.

In full regalia, I paraded around the living room, dragging the train of my new robe and proudly displaying my medal. When the Señor got his camera, I struck a pose for him. Since it is a newfangled digital camera, he can turn it around and push a button and show me the picture on the spot. My eyes widened as I gazed upon the likeness of myself.

Now I can add the initials R.A. after my name, becoming Sir Nobby R.A. It will look splendid on the stationary and business cards the Señor will be ordering for my correspondence. I will also put it on the new website.

A Sad Day

Every day cannot be sunny and bright. Some are gray and sad. After a glorious Christmas, the weather turned cold. And this morning the entire town and hillside to the east of us was covered with dark gray clouds. We don't have much humidity down here in the tropics, so there was no fog. But the thick clouds drifted low and kept the sun from shining through.

Since it was so drab, I stayed inside. I sat in an armchair and thought heavy thoughts about how I had been feeling low lately. Unlike Whiskers, who has been so full of life and fun, trying to entice me into running after her, I have been simply sitting around and thinking about myself. I have noticed that when people think too much about themselves, usually they begin to feel lowdown and sad. That's when a cat sings the blues, which is as much a state of mind as it is a trend of music. I like the blues sometimes, when a gutsy singer belts it out. A good blues singer can make down look like up to the person who is listening.

But on this day, everything seemed *blah*. I think I might have what humans call the "mid-life crisis." Now, don't get me wrong, I'm not depressed. It's just a spell I'm going through. I'm not ready for long-term old age or a retirement home. I'm not ready for a lap-blanket and a wheelchair. Not yet, anyway.

But sometimes I think about Nobby the First and how he just rolled himself up into a ball one morning, drifted into a nap and never woke up. It was a peaceful going away.

Today, I finally tell myself, I am not as old as Nobby the First was when he took his long nap. I've still got a spring to my step. I can still wink at Whiskers and rub my shoulder next to her soft side. I can make a purring sound that induces her to purr deep down in her own throat.

The very thought makes me frisky. I look outside and see a glimmer of light. A moment later the sun is shining bright as a July afternoon. I'm going to enjoy this day, I tell myself. I take a nice stroll through the garden, say hello to the rooster, pass Alfredo on the path. He says a brisk, "*Buenos dias, Nobby*," and I lift my head high. I smell the flowers that are blooming in the sun's brilliance. The sky suddenly turns a deep blue and the birds begin singing in the trees.

I find a hunk of tuna fish the Señor has put out for me and I gobble it down before lying down in the sun and closing my eyes for a great little catnap. What could be better? *Purr*haps a little later I will jump up onto the desk and go on-line, do a little computer drawing, maybe an abstract with many colors.

When I wake up, I look out at the sunshine. Feeling good, I brush myself down, comb out my whiskers, curl them just so, and straighten my coat and tie, imagining that I have such clothing. I sing a *meow*-song and do a little dance. While no one is looking, I daydream that Whiskers and I are doing a slinky Argentine tango.

I am such a happy cat. Isn't it wonderful what will happen if you just give yourself a little time? All you need to do is give yourself some time-out, be free and worryless, and time will take care of whatever might have been bothering you.

I feel so good, I amble over to the computer and plop my paws down on the keyboard. Because my song is still in my head I decide to do a little poem writing. I want to express some thoughts. At times like these the words flow like water from a spring.

A Cat is a Cat

A cat is a cat
and a mouse is a mouse;
but they can't live together
in the same house.

Forget the computer,
forget the TV,
and only remember
a cat that is me.
That's "meow" like me.
Forget all your worries,
just learn how to purr
and pat yourself softly,
like cats lick their fur.

NIGHT SERENADE

What are we doing
when we are all meowing
and howling and prowling
on the nights with full moon?
We're letting the world hear
if you scream loud and clear
you've got nothing to fear.
The moon will shine brighter,
the dark will get lighter,
and the ghosts will scamper,
and the daylight will come soon.

Famous Sir Nobby

It's almost too much to comprehend. I know that I was born of nobility. I have known that since the very beginning, when I learned about my ancestors coming from California, where they flitted around Hollywood, making movies. But lately, one honor after another has been falling my way. First, my painting was hung in the National Gallery, then I became an associate member of the Royal Academy, and the Señor draped the robe upon my shoulders and presented me with a diploma.

Now my photograph will hang in the Hall of Fame at the Cat Museum. I am told that I am now truly a famous feline. Here is a reproduction of that photograph, and I must say that I like it very much because it shows me as a very nice pusscat. I like to see my eyes. Cats can do tricks with their eyes. Do you know that cats can change the iris in their eyes from a mere slit to a wide circle? That's something humans can't do.

Watch your cat carefully. A cat can make many different expressions. We don't always look the same way all the time. That's another reason why, I believe, I could become a superior actor. If you are drawing a cat, observe what the eyes are doing. Watch very closely and you will see the change in expression.

I do not believe a dog or a rabbit can do that thing with their eyes.

Watch yours and see for yourself what I'm talking about.

Last summer, when a California cat was visiting next door, I tried some of my talent for changing expressions out on her. I think I impressed her, but she did act pretty snooty. I figured she would know about acting since she was from California. She was a good-looking little thing who knew how to twist and strut. But she wasn't quite my type.

Nobby's Note: Samantha and I didn't get along that well, but she was cute—and even slinky. When she asked me sweetly, I told her I'd let her write a few paragraphs for my memoir.

SAMANTHA THE BOMBSHELL

I'm a California cat. If you've never met one, you don't know what you're missing. I'm the "It Cat" the way Clara Bow used to be the "It Girl" of the motion picture world. When *Cats Illustrated* had a contest for Cover Cat of the Year, I was runner-up. I would have won, but the winner was a floozy cat who rubbed her Persian fur next to the director's side and purred sweet nothings to him.

I have heard that the uppity cat who calls himself "Sir Nobby" is writing about me. I hope he writes something nice, but I wouldn't stake my reputation on it. I was not very impressed with him. We California cats are very special and we live in a wonderful country. Many of us live there because we are in the movies. If you go to a cat-flick, you will more than likely see many of my friends on the silver screen. If you saw *Catalina Kitty Cat*, my friend Dolores was the star. She played beach blanket bingo with two very handsome actor-cats. If you look closely during the big beach scene, you might see me walking out of the water in my bikini. My friend Dolores put in a good word for me with the director, and, since I was runner-up in the *Cats Illustrated* cover girl contest, he thought it was a good idea to use me in the shot.

For that movie alone, Dolores made two thousand dollars. That's more than her owner-master

makes in a week of his work, and she's very proud of it. Next month she will appear in a Snippy Nippy Cat Food commercial on television. She'll be looking slinky and purring for the camera.

I must tell you, I do know how to look pretty. Even without make-up and careful brushing, I am what you might call one lovely-looking lady cat.

I know all the male cats like me, but I'm very standoffish. I won't go with just any old cat and I wouldn't shake my tail for that Sir Nobby, I can tell you that in a San Diego minute. Some day I will find the right cat for a husband. He won't be a Siamese. I'm looking for a dark and handsome gray cat who has a certain romantic quality in his demeanor and in his purr. He will know instinctively how much I like to go hiking in the woods near our house on the mountainside and he won't have to be a rat-catcher either. In fact, I'd pre*furr* a pleasant civilized intelligent California Tom who is comfortable with his position in the world.

I didn't meet anyone like that in Mexico. When my owner-master rented the house next door to the Señor, I talked with Whiskers about my situation. Of course, she tried to tell me the most erudite cat in the neighborhood was Sir Nobby, but I just shook my head. Then she advised me to learn some Spanish *meow*-talk and I would understand the San Miguel cats much better, but I figured they should learn my own Californian *meow*-talk. Why should I stoop?

Now I'm happy to be back in California. Dolores and I may go to the mall in the valley and do some cat shopping. Here, I don't have to worry about Sir Nobby. If he writes bad things about me,

I'll sue. People in California sue writers if they publish bad things about them. With the help of Dolores, I'll find a good cat-lawyer and sue that uppity Siamese.

In the meantime, I've heard talk that I've been seen by the right people in my walk-on role on the beach. I've gotten rave notices in *Cat Chic*, the *People* of the cat world. A photo showed me having champagne with Tom Paw, the heartthrob of feline films, and he was even quoted in "*Purr*fect Paws," the gossip column, as saying I was "the bombshell of the modern cat cinema." The people in the know apparently are very impressed with my swinging tail and my erect posture. When a television exec came for lunch with my master, he said, "What a lovely looking cat you have. She looks familiar. Has she been in anything lately?" And when my man named the movie and the role, the exec said, "We could use her sometimes, if you'll let us. Could you give us a call?"

So *purr*haps I'll meet a real cat friend and have a husband and some nice little California kittens. Maybe I won't have to sue, after all.

FIESTAS

I've heard that Mexicans will use any excuse to have a fiesta and I believe it. They love to take a day off from work, have a big party, organize a parade, set off firecrackers morning, noon, night, and morning again. A big part of having a good time is playing music and dancing and whooping loudly. Mexicans are generally a happy-go-lucky people. They work hard between fiestas, then they play just as hard.

San Miguel is a great fiesta town. Every neighborhood has its own special day for a fiesta. They collect firecrackers and fire off rockets that go bang in the night. Since I have been in Mexico all of my life, I am quite accustomed to the loud blasts that sound like a new revolution practically every week. Now and then we will have a visitor in one of the houses near us. If it's a cat or dog from the United States, they are very often frightened by the loud explosions. If I have the chance, I explain that it is no big deal; it's simply the Mexican way of life.

On a child's birthday, the special treat is a *piñata*. A thin clay pot is filled with fruit and candy. Often, the clay pot is covered with paper. At Christmas, the paper is usually red and green and gold, all glittery and beautiful. Sometimes the *piñata* is shaped like a star or small person or a bird or a dog or cat. It is always colorful. The *piñata* is tied to a rope and suspended from a high place. It is then lifted just high enough for the children to reach it with a wooden

bat. At birthday parties the child is often blindfolded, turned around and around, then steadied in front of the *piñata.* He or she then strikes toward the object, usually missing the first few times, causing those in attendance to laugh and giggle. When the child finally smashes the *piñata,* all of the goodies tumble out and scatter across the floor or yard. The children rush for the goodies, all the goodies they can reach.

It is great fun. The Mexicans—young and old—enjoy the good time. No one gets hurt. There's some healthy teasing. And everybody enjoys the sweets.

The Señor was having a *piñata* party for one of the neighbor's children one afternoon when I saw my first balloon. Not a small rubber balloon filled with gas and carried in the hands of children. And not a large paper balloon that local people send up with a lighted candle inside that floats high into the nighttime sky and shines like a colored star. I'm talking about a huge balloon with gas attachments and a basket attached to the bottom and a pilot to keep it on course. Only this afternoon the pilot miscalculated the distance. I watched it sweep overhead. As it came closer and closer, I called out to Scruffy, Florence, and Whiskers to hide as quickly as possible. I ran for Alfredo's studio, hiding under the wide eave.

The hot-air balloon, making a loud swishing sound, soared overhead and looked as though it was about to drop into our garden. Whiskers and Scruffy ran for cover. Florence was left behind. But she soon found her way into the Señor's house.

The children were all scrambling for safety. The Señor grabbed several and held them close to his side. The balloon was losing altitude fast, and heading straight toward our garden. I held my breath as it swept low. When it dipped down, the bottom of the basket caught on the high limb of a tree in the far end of our garden. It hesitated. Would it topple over and crash? The children gasped audibly.

Suddenly a loud whooshing sound came from the balloon. It broke free of the limb, jerked upward into the sky, and flew past the garden to land in a field down the road. A few minutes later, the pilot and passengers knocked on our door and came into the house, apologizing for frightening everyone. The pilot explained that when sudden winds come up, a hot-air balloon is difficult to control. It can be very dangerous.

That day, everyone was safe. It scared all the cats. And it scared the children as well. We all watched as the air went out of the balloon. It was folded and put in the back of a truck and hauled away. No one volunteered for a free ride.

Later, when I saw the hot-air balloon sailing high above San Miguel with tourists aboard, I wondered if they knew just how dangerous such a ride could be. They can have their fun. It's beautiful up there. But I know at least three cats who decline to see the sights in such a dramatic way.

Whiskers and Scruffy and I have often talked among ourselves about the possibilities of having a cat *piñata*. Perhaps next year on Florence's birthday. It would be wonderful if the Señor would find some cat goodies to put into the clay pot. Maybe smoked salmon, or nice pieces of fish or shrimp. Not candies and fruit, which we do not eat. It would be something special, just for us.

The next time I'm on the Internet, I'll ask the question. *Purr*haps there are other cats out there somewhere who know where we may find such delicacies. And it would add so much to our own Mexican parties.

Cat-Tel

As she grows older, Whiskers is becoming a wise lady cat, or *La Gata*, as she is known around the *colonia*. She has gotten more and more beautiful as she matures. Her whiskers are very white now and most distinguished. She carries herself with dignity. If I didn't know better, I would think she's royalty.

When I told her about the Internet Conference I was planning, she said simply, "Walk before you run." Her words made me think. The computer idea is good but complicated. *Why not try to communicate first by telephone? It would be much simpler, don't you think?*

Everyone walks about with pocket-sized telephones in their purses or pockets. Even little children have them. They lose them too. People find them in the street or left behind in restaurants and cafés. They are easy to operate. If we could have one to try out and get ourselves a *meow*-number, we'd be in business. It would begin our communications program. Everything is so automatic these days it should be easy to get a *meow*-number listed with the telephone office.

The richest billionaire in Mexico owns telephone and computer companies. *Purr*haps he would help us animals if we could let him know that we'd like to start a Cat-Tel operation. I don't know how we'd pay the bill, but *purr*haps he is a cat and dog lover and would do something for us in the new age we are all living in. It would be quite an innovation in this modern world. And it's worth trying, I think. I'll bring the idea up when we have our conference.

Don't be surprised if one day the phone meows instead of rings. You might pick up the receiver and hear "Meow? Meow? Who is it?" *Vamos a ver*—wait and see, as we say in Mexico.

ANTS

lthough I do worry and try to think of ways to solve great problems, deep inside I am a Zen cat. As such, I study our surroundings here in the garden to discover what I am sure exists somewhere out in the universe beyond our walls. For instance, lately I have been watching the ants who live in the dirt of the garden. Theirs is an amazing society. When you first see them, they look as though they are running helter-skelter without a worry in the world and with no thought to details. However, if you watch closely, you will begin to see that what appears to be total chaos is precise order. Each ant is carrying out his or her duty. Each knows exactly what he or she is doing, and they are doing their chores for the benefit of the entire community. Sometimes they travel a great distance from their home to the field where they are doing their work.

The ruler is the Queen. Elected by the entire population, she is at the top of the order. Beneath her are officer ants in the chain of command. They are responsible for making sure her orders are carried out. And then there are hundreds—even thousands—of worker ants. There are cutter ants who cut leaves from trees and stack them up, carrier ants who pick up the leaves and carry them all the way back to the home base, hunter ants who go out on missions to find food supplies and report back to the officers, warrior ants who fight the wars with other unfriendly ants or attack animals who try to destroy their home, and homebody ants who tend to the storage, the care and the feeding, first of the Queen and then the rest of the tribe. It is amazing—and extraordinarily educational—to sit and watch this culture carrying on the ant tradition that has been handed down from generation to generation and which does not vary from anthill to anthill.

To the Señor, ants are pests. He tries to rid the garden of them. I have watched him spray a colony at the entrance to their hole in the earth. Once, when hundreds of flying ants emerged and appeared on the wall of his bedroom, the Señor sprayed them with a vengeance. What amazes me is the fact that they keep coming back. Those homebody ants—other than carrying out their duties of storing food—store a great supply of ant eggs deep down in the ground. After the Señor or another human sprays the ants—or after a great battle between ant tribes, such as ones I have witnessed night after night in the kitchen—the eggs burst open and thousands of new ants appear, almost like magic. They know instinctively that they will be replaced by more ants. It is obviously a part of their lifecycle that they understand: the worker ants, soldier ants, lieutenants and homebodies, and even the mighty Queen might be killed in an instant, but just as quickly they will be replaced by offspring that have been stored as eggs deep inside their world.

In studying the ant world we learn the lesson of life itself. Even though Tabby is gone, the rest of us cats at the Señor's house in San Miguel live on— the same way the ant world survives, even after humans spray them with the most powerful poison in a can.

NEW YEAR

The New Year is here. Everyone is celebrating. Last night revelers brought in the New Year by crowding into the *jardin* or central plaza in the center of San Miguel. As the bells of *La Parroquia* church struck twelve times, everyone cheered. People toasted, hugged, kissed, and lit firecrackers that sounded all the way to the Señor's house.

Cats don't keep calendars, but we know about time. And we can tell when the people of our world celebrate the beginning of a new year. Sometimes they go crazy with it, drinking too much and screaming too loud. We know that there is a difference between the celebrations of Christmas and of the New Year. In this town, where there is a celebration for almost anything you might imagine, a cat is careful about when he goes outside the comfort and security of his own home garden. If you're not careful, you might get caught up in a celebration in the street and swept along with the crowd and its noise.

Also, I am aware of the passing of time. I know I am getting older and older. As people celebrate, we cats have our own quiet celebration. On New Year's Day I rubbed my fur next to Florence, I put my nose close to Scruffy, and I told Whiskers I thought she was getting prettier and prettier every day. They all responded with loving instincts.

After all, when you share a garden and a house, you need to be close and caring. It's something that makes me feel better, letting them know how much I care for them.

Whiskers tells me that her philosophy is to live from day to day. I nod and contemplate her words. She says I shouldn't worry about what happens tomorrow. Tomorrow will take care of itself. She picked up such thoughts from our Mexican friends, who say in Spanish, "*Pan y toros, y manana es un otra dia.*" Bread and bulls, and tomorrow is another day. Eat and have a good time at the fiesta today, tomorrow is another time. Shrug a good cat shrug and go on with life.

So, on this New Year's Day, I tell my cat friends, "Let's count our blessings." After the first morning's hug, we begin having our fun, running with the roosters and chickens, who cackle but are not hurt. Scruffy joined us in the fun, and we all meowed, "Happy New Year," the way the Señor and his friends greet each other.

SURPRISE

n the first week of the new year, the Señor received a package in the mail. It was postmarked Washington D.C.

I tried to be calm, but I jumped onto the sofa next to the Señor and rubbed next to his arm and tried to push my nose into the package. But the Señor pushed me away and said, "I'll open it in a minute, Nobby."

I climbed onto the back of the sofa where I could watch him rip open the manila envelope. He slid his hand inside. Out came a perfect replica of the painting he had sent north a month earlier. But it had been shaped and slicked with little niches in each corner and $1 added to the right bottom.

"Look at this!" the Señor exclaimed with a big smile. "Sir Nobby, you will be even more famous than your predecessor. There will be hundreds of thousands of Sir Nobby stamps sold in every post office in the United States. Every time a special package needing a one-dollar stamp is sent to Mexico, your face will be on it. Isn't that wonderful?" His voice lilted as it does when he's excited about something.

I meowed my appreciation and couldn't take my eyes off the picture of the stamp.

Now, of course, I will be more famous than ever! And it comes right when I had decided it might be best to be a regular old pusscat. I had made up my mind I would be happy being a nobody, living a quiet life with my cat friends in the safety of my garden. A nice simple life, that's all I want. But isn't that when everything changes for cats or humans? Right when we decide that fame isn't worth it, that's

when it pours down on top of our heads. If I'd sought fame, the way I did when I was young, being jealous of Nobby the First because he was so well known around the world, I would have been forgotten. Now, here I am on the verge of the biggest notoriety ever. It is so funny. Now I would just as soon be known only by the Señor, his circle of friends, and my buddies in the garden. They are all great and love me for what I am, not because of some silly image on a stamp.

Now, even before my book is published, people want to see me. They come to the house and talk to the Señor. He points me out and they aim their cameras at me. I get e-mail letters and the phone rings. The Señor is tired of people asking questions, wanting to know all about me. Reporters come to the house and interview the Señor about me. They want to know everything I did before I became a celebrity with my image on a popular stamp in the United States.

And now that the word has leaked about me writing my memoirs, *People* and *Us* are interested in cover stories. Only yesterday the phone rang. A journalist from New York asked the Señor several questions and he slammed the receiver down. Afterwards, he said he would answer no more questions.

I feel badly about all this. I want to go and hide. I want to be with Scruffy and Whiskers and Florence. I wish we had a dog. A big, mean dog who would tear the pants off of any photographer who came sneaking around the garden.

I have to confess, however, that I have only myself to blame. When it came down to these last pages of my memoir, I got the bright idea that I should have an ample amount of publicity. I mean, what's an autobiography without hype? Right? Well, it was I who was fooling around on the computer several weeks ago, tiptoeing across the Internet, when I clicked onto the *New York Times*. Well, I not only got onto the *Times* website, I discovered how to contact the Culture Editor. I began working fast, making sure my message was sent before the Señor found me on his computer. I told my story: how I was a little Siamese who had been found by the Señor at the ranch near Tampico and how he'd brought me to the wonderful art colony of San Miguel de Allende where he was a famous artist. Then I told about how the Señor had painted me and the U.S. government had chosen me to appear on the special one-dollar stamp and how I was now writing my most interesting memoirs.

I not only sent my message to the Culture Editor, I copied it to editors of at least a half-dozen magazines, including *People* and *Us*. So, I guess the Señor should be aiming his displeasure at me.

TABBY

After Tabby disappeared, we heard he'd been run over by a car. But I never said a word to Florence about that. After his disappearance, Florence looked everywhere for her Tabby but couldn't find him. She went into a funk and stayed depressed for a long while. Scruffy and I did tricks, trying to make her happy, but all our efforts failed.

Time passed. Christmas came. Florence tried her best to be cheery. She even smiled once or twice when the children played their *piñata* game, shouting and laughing. Then New Years came and we had pieces of turkey the Señor gave us on the special day. That made Florence smile. But mostly she just sat around and stared up into the sky. Now and then I'd see her eyes look toward the wall. I knew she was hoping to see her Tabby climb over in the middle of the morning, coming back from his nighttime carousing, like he used to do.

After spring came and the days got longer and brighter, we were all lounged out on the patio late one morning when we heard a strange *meow*. I opened my eyes and glanced over at Florence. When I looked out toward where the rooster lives, I saw this tabby cat walking toward us. When he stepped forward on his right front foot, he limped. His eyes were slightly shaded. There was a scar across his chest where his fur had once been ripped open, then had healed on its own.

"Tabby?" I asked.

He looked at me with an older, wiser expression than I remembered on the old Tabby's face.

Florence raised her head, staring in his direction. "Tabby?" she asked. "My Tabby?"

Tabby nodded. He did not stop. He limped directly to her and lowered his head to hers. He rubbed his chin across her neck and purred deep down in his throat.

For a moment, I thought Florence was going to lose it. She answered his loving gesture with her own. "Tabby, where on earth have you been?" she asked.

After we all settled down and Tabby had eaten and lapped up an ample amount of water, he told us about being run over by a truck down on the Ancha San Antonio. "When I awakened, I was lying in a ditch next to the highway. The collision had torn the front of my body, ripping open my chest. There was a throbbing pain in my head. When I tried to open my eyes, I discovered my right eye had been torn from the socket. I could barely see out of my left. I didn't know where I was or what had happened to me," he said.

He had bled so much he was very weak. A ranchero with a burro picked him up, carried him to his shack somewhere near the road to Celaya. The farmer plied Tabby's wounds with a grease mixture he used on his work animals. He fixed a hot compress that he put into the wound where Tabby's right eye had once been. Little by little, Tabby managed to gain some of his strength. The ranchero gave him milk and some scraps from his own meager table. Tabby lived under a lean-to with the burro who would lick his fur at night and try to make him comfortable.

Finally, after months with the farmer, he followed him and the burro into town one day. They were delivering firewood to one of the big houses in the Centro. After three trips into town, Tabby spotted a street that looked familiar. "I didn't want to appear

ungrateful to the ranchero. He was a poor man who had been good to me. And the burro had been very kind and caring," Tabby said. But he missed his Florence more than anything in the world, so finally he broke away from his new family and followed the street that eventually led him to our *callejon*, where he recognized the wall and decided to give it a try. Now, here he was, back with his old friends and his loving Florence, who said she didn't care if he didn't have but one eye, she loved him no matter how he looked. They cuddled in the corner of the patio, where he told her he would never leave her again.

With that thought on my mind, I closed my eyes and drifted into a sleep. I knew I would dream good dreams.

JUST PLAIN NOBBY

As I grow older, all the certificates of recognition, such as my knighthood, and all the fame, like having my likeness spread all over the world on a postage stamp, mean less and less. *You know what really means something?* Having the Señor looking after me, having great friends like Florence and Tabby, Whiskers and Scruffy. They are my world, not those fickle writers and photographers who come down from Toronto or New York. All of them sit and talk to the Señor, who tells them wonderfully interesting stories about my cat's life. He tells them they will be able to read about it soon in my memoirs, which he is now editing.

They *ooh* and *aah* over me. The photographers want me to pose. I look at them out of my slanted eyes—the ones I told you about earlier. But they don't get it. And I haven't found a writer yet who knows how to ask a question in *meow*-talk, much less one who understands my answers.

When the intruders come, I whisper to the others to play-like they are taking a nap. "If we don't move, they'll go away," I tell my friends.

Sure enough, pretty soon the Señor chuckles and says, "Well, I don't think he's up to a pose today." He knows I'm playing possum, but it rather amuses him. He too knows the cost of fame. When he became a great artist, recognized by authorities in his homeland of Canada and in New York and on the West Coast, he enjoyed the fame up to a point, but he soon tired of all of the nonsense of cameras being shoved into his face and journalists probing through the details of his life. And when he was given a one-man show at the Bellas Artes de Nacional in Mexico City (which is highly unusual for artists who are not native to Mexico), his picture was in every paper in the country, and some of the most renowned experts proclaimed him The Maestro. It was all very good, his paintings sold for top prices—but after it was all said and done, he came back here to San Miguel. He strolled in the garden with us and told us we were his favorite animals in the whole world. "I wouldn't trade you for anything they've got in the big capital city," he said. "You are my pride and joy."

I was very happy. The Señor did not single me out because I had nobility. Noble, catoble, I'm just plain old Nobby, a cat who loves his Señor and his friends. I don't try to paint nowadays. After I was accepted into the Royal Academy, I asked myself: *Why continue? You've accomplished a great goal.* No need to compete with the Señor. He is the great artist, not I. And I've even given up the computer. Now and then I do a dance on the piano keyboard, but it's all in fun—just to show the others I can do it. We all have fun. It's all in the family. I push my face against Florence's cheek and she purrs deep down. Out of the corner of my eye I see Tabby raise his brows, a touch of jealousy rippling beneath his fur, but he knows I'm just old Nobby showing that I love them all. That's all I need to be to make my life full and rich.

As far as I can tell, I have the *purr*fect life.

CAT LIT

I know you are a lover of literature or you wouldn't be reading my miraculous memoirs. I am also a student of the written word. I read the Señor's books when he leaves them open on his desk. I go onto the Internet and search for caterific catalogues. I ever *purr*use the magazines for stories about people and animals.

Just the other day I was reading about the new trend called "Chick Lit" wherein the hero of the story is a woman with plenty of brains and enough good looks to win over any male who might cross her path. Well, I think that I am beginning a new trend. It will be called "Cat Lit." And I am sure every high-class magazine, the *New York Times*, the *Washington Post*, and all of the other really with-it newspapers from the *Toronto Star* to the *Times* of London will take notice.

And imagine, you are among the first to experience the true depth of Cat Lit. I know you'll go out and tell your friends. They will all pick up my little book and enjoy my cat stories.

AND WHERE IS SIR NOBBY?

The gallant Sir Nobby
has gone off to Mars
to be with the stars.
The first cat to go there,
the space station states;
"It's his destiny," so say the Fates.
No other like him,
this Siamese cat,
so nod and bow
as we give him a happy "Meow!"

P.S. Nothing wrong with dreaming, is there?

An Abrazo for Leonard Brooks, Artist, 95 on November 7, 2006
by Wayne Greenhaw

An *abrazo* for my friend Leonard,
whose bones are frail and brittle.
Voice raspy, eyes bright and gray,
he pulls out paintings to display,
works unfinished while I was away.
A flicker of white against the sky,
a bird in flight over San Miguel.
"Quebrada, where we used to live,"
he points to a spot where angles collide.
An illness lingers, a touch of bronchitis.
But it has not kept him from working,
adding a burro here, a ranchero there,
putting rain into the sky, a bird
over *iglesia* San Francisco, a tree
near a walkway in *la parque.*

The slender shoulder where a violin
once rested, now sags, as he lifts a finger

to purple bougainvillea in a courtyard,
an added touch that has come to mind.
Surrounded here on *calle* Quinta
by the lush rewards of a rich life,
from an orange and blue and gold tapestry
woven by a short-fingered Indian artisan
from one of Leonard's exact designs
to the street scenes of San Miguel
through the ninety more years of his life.
"As I walk the quay in Paris in the 20s
so do I stand near the market on *Mesones*
in the spring of 1955."

His life generates art as he recalls WW2.
Disguised as a war artist in the Royal Navy,
his words do not quiver as he remembers
standing down an insolent Nazi u-boat officer,
demanding the removal of a swastika
from his spit-and-polished uniform.
Leonard smiles. "I had to do that, you know."

I know. I've stood with him in the hallway,
where Reva's black-and-white photographs
are displayed in simple black frames.
A little boy lies in repose with unseeing eyes.
A paper crown is balanced on the baby's head.
A mother's sparkling, tearful eyes reflect
the majesty of a proud, undying race.

Leonard's finger reaches up, touches the glass
covering the ageless image, barely touching,
like the slight flicker of a brush against canvas.

WAYNE GREENHAW is the award-winning author of more than seventeen books, including *King of Country* and *The Thunder of Angels: The Montgomery Bus Boycott and the People Who Broke the Back of Jim Crow*. This poetic *abrazo* is from his collection *Ghosts on the Road: Poems of Alabama, Mexico, and Beyond*. He, his wife Sally, and their Havanese Ellie divide their time between Montgomery, Alabama, and San Miguel de Allende, Mexico. In addition to being a dear friend to Leonard Brooks, Wayne is also a close associate of Sir Nobby himself.